Table of Contents

Chimeras and Chapels

Catholic Ethics in Genetic Controversies

by

Dr. ant

Although the author and publisher have made every effort to ensure that the information in this book was correct at press time, the author and publisher do not assume and hereby disclaim any liability to any party for any loss, damage, or disruption caused by errors or omissions, whether such errors or omissions result from negligence, accident, or any other cause.

This publication is designed to provide accurate and authoritative information with regard to the subject matter covered. It is sold with the understanding that the publisher is not engaged in rendering professional services. If legal advice or other expert assistance is required, the services of a competent professional should be sought.

Chimeras and Chapels: Catholic Ethics in Genetic Controversies

Contents

Introduction: Navigating Genetic Frontiers Through the Lens of Catholic Ethics

The rapid advancement of genetic technologies, epitomized by breakthroughs such as CRISPR-Cas9, in vitro fertilization (IVF), and gametogenesis, marks a pivotal juncture in the annals of human civilization. These developments promise unprecedented benefits, including the potential eradication of hereditary diseases, enhanced agricultural yields, and new frontiers in reproductive health. Yet, they also pose profound ethical dilemmas, particularly within the framework of Catholic ethics, which prizes the sanctity of life, the natural order, and the intrinsic dignity of the human being.

This introduction seeks to set the stage for a comprehensive exploration of how Catholic ethics intersects with modern genetic technologies. In doing so, it will illuminate the guiding principles of Catholic bioethics, offer a critical examination of the moral and ethical implications of genetic engineering, and propose paths forward that respect both scientific progress and moral teachings.

The Catholic Church has long engaged with scientific inquiry, advocating for the harmony of faith and reason. As such, Catholic bioethics does not reflexively oppose scientific advances; rather, it seeks to evaluate them in light of enduring moral principles. Central to this evaluation is the intrinsic dignity of the human person, created in the image of God and endowed with inherent worth from conception to natural death.

Genetic engineering technology, particularly CRISPR-Cas9, offers a vivid illustration of the ethical challenges at hand. This technology enables precise editing of the genetic code, holding the potential for groundbreaking treatments and possibly even the elimination of genetic diseases. Yet, it also raises critical questions regarding the manipulation of human life, with far-reaching implications for our understanding of disease, health, and the essence of human nature itself.

Similarly, the advent of IVF and gametogenesis as means of aiding reproduction presents both blessings and ethical conundrums. While they provide hope to countless individuals facing infertility, they also prompt serious reflection on the beginning of life, the meaning of parenthood, and the commodification of human embryos.

The potential for genetic technologies to pave the way towards eugenics and the creation of 'designer babies' compounds these ethical concerns, compelling us to confront questions of equality, human diversity, and the very definition of perfection. The quest for genetically 'perfect' offspring not only challenges the principle of unconditional love but also risks reducing human beings to a set of desirable traits, thereby undermining their intrinsic worth.

Moreover, the disparate access to these genetic technologies illuminates issues of social justice, echoing the Church's teaching on the preferential option for the poor and the vulnerable. The risk of creating genetic disparities between the affluent and the marginalized raises significant concerns about equity, common good, and the moral imperative to ensure that scientific advancements benefit all of humanity.

The environmental implications of genetic engineering, especially in agriculture, further demonstrate the necessity of a comprehensive ethical analysis. The manipulation of genetic codes in plants and animals not only affects biodiversity but also poses unforeseeable risks to ecosystems. Here, the Catholic emphasis on stewardship of Creation comes to the fore, challenging us to consider the long-term consequences of our technological endeavors on the natural world.

In response to these complex issues, this book aims to provide a nuanced exploration of genetic technologies through the lens of Catholic ethics. It does not purport to offer easy answers; rather, it seeks to foster informed, thoughtful dialogue among Roman Catholics, ethicists, and university professors. Through this dialogue, it aims to contribute to the development of ethical guidelines that dignify the human person, respect the natural order, and promote the common good.

As we embark on this exploration, it is crucial to remember that Catholic bioethics is not static but dynamic, evolving in response to new scientific knowledge and societal changes. Thus, this examination is not only about critiquing contemporary moral issues but also about envisioning a future where genetic technologies are harnessed for the authentic betterment of humanity, in alignment with moral and ethical principles that transcend transient trends.

In conclusion, navigating the genetic frontiers requires wisdom, prudence, and compassion. As we delve into this complex terrain, let us be guided by a commitment to uphold human dignity, a dedication to justice, and a fervent hope in the possibility of harnessing scientific progress for the true flourishing of all individuals and society at large. It is within this spirit that we undertake our inquiry into the intersection of genetic technologies and Catholic ethics, charting a course that honors both human ingenuity and the timeless values that define us as moral beings.

Chapter 3: Foundations of Catholic Bioethics

In the labyrinth of contemporary ethical dilemmas brought forth by advances in biotechnology, such as CRISPR, gametogenesis, and in vitro fertilization, the compass of Catholic bioethics remains steadfastly oriented towards the sanctity and dignity of human life. Grounded in a rich tapestry of theological, philosophical, and moral principles, Catholic bioethics serves not only as a response to the rapid pace of scientific progress but also as a proactive guide in navigating the complex moral landscapes these technologies present. At the heart of this ethical framework is a profound respect for the inherent worth of every human being, a concept that profoundly shapes the Church's approach to contemporary bioethical issues. This foundational principle is supported by a nuanced understanding of natural law, which asserts that moral norms can be discerned through reason and the natural inclinations of human beings towards certain fundamental goods, including life itself. Furthermore, the principle of double effect, a critical tool in Catholic moral reasoning, offers a way to evaluate actions that can have both good and bad outcomes, allowing for a careful discernment of ethical choices in complex medical and scientific scenarios. This chapter delves into these foundational elements, elucidating how they inform and guide the Church's stance on the pressing bioethical issues of our time, ensuring that the march of scientific progress is matched with a profound moral responsibility towards the sacredness of life.

The Dignity of Human Life: Catholic Perspectives

In the discourse of Catholic bioethics, the dignity of human life stands as a cornerstone principle, guiding the moral evaluation of biotechnological advancements such as CRISPR, gametogenesis, and in vitro fertilization. The essence of this dignity is anchored in the belief that each person is created imago Dei, in the image of God, which imbues every stage of human life with intrinsic worth and sacredness.

This intrinsic worth extends from conception to natural death, setting a framework within which Catholics approach bioethical issues. It compels us to consider not just the scientific possibilities but the moral implications of actions that affect human life. As technologies like gene editing present unprecedented opportunities, they also challenge us to question how these innovations align with the preservation of human dignity.

The penetration of CRISPR-Cas9 technology into the fabric of genetic research offers a vivid example of this tension. While the potential for disease eradication and genetic improvement is significant, the ethical considerations rooted in Catholic teaching prompt a careful analysis of the means and ends. The sanctity of life, in this context, serves as a beacon, illuminating the ethical paths that respect human dignity while embracing beneficial progress.

Similarly, the advent of techniques such as in vitro fertilization (IVF) and gametogenesis raises complex moral dilemmas. While acknowledging the profound desire for parenthood that drives individuals toward these technologies, Catholic bioethics evaluates these methods through the lens of human dignity, questioning their implications for the sanctity of the procreative process and the respect due to the nascent human life.

At the heart of these bioethical evaluations is a commitment to the common good, a principle that transcends individual desires and aims for the holistic welfare of society. This commitment challenges the notion of autonomy when it comes to decisions affecting new human lives and the genetic makeup of future generations. In this light, Catholic bioethics advocates for a reasoned discernment that weighs scientific advancements against their potential to undermine the inherent dignity of human life.

The Catholic perspective on bioethics also engages with the moral evils associated with practices like eugenics and the creation of "designer babies." These endeavors, aimed at enhancing human traits through genetic manipulation, are critically assessed for their potential to commodify human life and exacerbate social inequalities. The Church's teaching calls for an unequivocal rejection of such practices, emphasizing the equal dignity of all human lives, regardless of their genetic attributes.

Moreover, the Church's stance on healthcare and genetics underlines the preferential option for the poor, reminding us that the benefits of genetic medicine should be accessible to all, rather than exacerbating existing disparities. This focus on social justice extends to the field of agricultural biotechnology, where genetic engineering's implications for the environment and food security are scrutinized through the lens of stewardship and care for creation.

At the intersection of faith and reason, Catholic bioethics does not reject the advances of science outright but calls for a harmonious integration of scientific progress with moral principles. This approach seeks not to hinder scientific exploration but to ensure that such endeavors are oriented toward the authentic good of humanity, respecting the dignity of human life at every turn.

The ethical landscape of biotechnology is ever-evolving, and as such, the Catholic Church's engagement with bioethical issues is dynamic. Through constant dialogue with the scientific community, theologians, and ethicists, the Church aims to contribute a moral voice that is both informed and prophetic, shedding light on the path that honors both human dignity and God's creation.

In this complex interplay between genetic science and moral theology, Catholic bioethics serves as a thoughtful mediator, advocating for an approach that is both open to innovation and deeply rooted in ethical principles. It challenges society to not only ask what we can do but more importantly, what we ought to do in our stewardship of the gift of human life.

As we stand on the brink of new genetic frontiers, the Catholic Church remains a steadfast guardian of the principle that every human life is precious. It is an unshakeable commitment to human dignity that shapes the Catholic response to bioethical challenges, guiding us through the moral intricacies of our technological age.

In conclusion, the Catholic understanding of the dignity of human life provides a vital perspective in the discourse on bioethics, offering a moral compass that navigates through the tumultuous seas of scientific advancement. It reminds us that at the heart of all bioethical inquiries should be a profound respect for the sacredness of human life, a respect that informs and directs our choices in the realm of genetic technology.

Moral Principles in Catholic Teaching

The exploration of moral principles within Catholic teaching provides a cornerstone for addressing the complex issues that emerge at the intersection of faith and the rapidly evolving field of genetic engineering. The Catholic tradition offers a rich tapestry of ethical considerations that are particularly relevant when confronting contemporary moral dilemmas surrounding CRISPR, gametogenesis, and in vitro fertilization. These moral principles are not just abstract concepts but are deeply rooted in the belief in the sanctity of human life and the inherent dignity of every person.

Central to Catholic bioethics is the understanding that every human being is created in the image and likeness of God. This foundational belief informs the church's approach to all questions of life and death, influencing its stance on cutting-edge genetic technologies. The application of these technologies, while holding the promise of significant medical breakthroughs, also poses ethical challenges that require careful discernment.

The principle of respect for life guides the Catholic approach to bioethics. This principle asserts that all human life, from conception to natural death, possesses inherent dignity and value. The implications of this for genetic engineering are profound. Technologies such as CRISPR and IVF must be evaluated not only on their scientific merit but also on their ability to uphold the dignity of human life in all its stages.

Catholic bioethics also emphasizes the moral principle of doing good and avoiding evil. This principle, while seemingly straightforward, involves complex considerations in the context of genetic engineering. For instance, while the potential to eradicate genetic diseases through CRISPR technology represents a significant good, the unintended consequences or misuse of such technology could result in considerable harm. Thus, the moral imperative to do good requires a balanced consideration of both the benefits and risks associated with genetic interventions.

The notion of the common good further shapes the Catholic ethical perspective. In the realm of genetic engineering, this principle urges the scientific community and society at large to consider how advancements in genetics can benefit not only individuals but society as a whole. This includes evaluating the accessibility of genetic therapies and ensuring that the benefits of genetic research are shared equitably. The preferential option for the poor, a key element of Catholic social teaching, is particularly relevant in this regard. It challenges the scientific and medical communities to prioritize treatments and interventions that address the needs of the most vulnerable populations.

Freedom and responsibility are also vital components of Catholic bioethics. While individuals are endowed with the freedom to make choices, this freedom is not absolute but must be exercised responsibly, particularly when those choices have the potential to impact human life and dignity profoundly. In the context of genetic engineering, this principle prompts serious reflection on the ethical implications of human actions and the responsibility to use scientific knowledge wisely and for the greater good.

The principle of stewardship compels Catholics to consider their role as caretakers of God's creation. This includes a moral obligation to respect the natural order and to use scientific knowledge to promote human flourishing without compromising the integrity of the natural world. In debates surrounding genetic manipulation, this principle highlights the need for caution and humility, recognizing the limits of human knowledge and the potential long-term consequences of altering the genetic fabric of living organisms.

Integral to Catholic teaching is the principle of solidarity, which emphasizes the interconnectedness of all people. This principle has profound implications for genetic engineering, particularly in fostering global cooperation to address ethical challenges and ensure that advances in genetics serve the common good of humanity, transcending national, economic, and social divides.

In conclusion, the moral principles embedded in Catholic teaching provide a framework for engaging with the ethical challenges posed by genetic engineering. These principles, grounded in a profound respect for life and human dignity, call for a thoughtful and measured approach to the development and application of genetic technologies. They remind us that, amidst the promise of scientific advancement, we must remain vigilant guardians of the moral values that define our humanity.

Natural Law and Its Role in Ethical Decision-Making As we delve further into the complexities of bioethics within the sphere of genetic engineering, it becomes imperative to understand the foundational principles guiding moral discernment in this area. Among these principles, natural law stands out as a critical framework, especially within Catholic ethical tradition. This section aims to explore natural law's pivotal role in ethical decision-making as it relates to contemporary moral issues such as CRISPR, gametogenesis, and in vitro fertilization.

Natural law theory posits that moral principles are derived from the inherent nature of humans and the physical and moral order of the universe. These principles, accessible through human reason, provide a universal standard for distinguishing right from wrong. In the context of genetic engineering, natural law compels us to ask fundamental questions about the purpose and limits of human intervention in the natural order.

The principle of the sanctity of human life is a cornerstone of natural law ethics. It asserts the inherent value and dignity of every human person, irrespective of their physical, genetic, or social attributes. This principle challenges the ethical permissibility of technologies like CRISPR and in vitro fertilization, prompting a careful consideration of how these technologies respect or violate the intrinsic worth of human life.

Another crucial aspect of natural law is the concept of telos, or purpose. According to natural law, everything in nature has a purpose or end to which it is ordered. This teleological perspective raises important questions in the ethical evaluation of genetic engineering. Do these technologies align with the natural purposes of human existence and reproduction, or do they represent a manipulation of nature's design?

Gametogenesis, the process of creating gametes outside the human body, presents a particularly challenging case for ethical analysis under natural law. By separating procreation from the marital act, gametogenesis raises significant concerns about the natural purpose of reproduction and the rights of the unborn.

In vitro fertilization (IVF), while offering hope to many couples facing infertility, also invites scrutiny under natural law. The creation and often subsequent destruction of embryos in the IVF process pose profound ethical dilemmas about the respect owed to human life at its earliest stages and the natural context in which human life should be conceived and nurtured.

The potential for CRISPR technology to edit the human genome presents unprecedented ethical challenges. While the promise of curing genetic diseases is laudable, the manipulation of the genetic makeup of humans raises profound questions about the respect for the natural genetic endowment of individuals and the species as a whole. Natural law ethics compel us to consider the limits of human dominion over nature and the morality of altering fundamental aspects of human identity.

Amid these technological advances, natural law provides a crucial ethical lens through which to view the dignity of human life, the purposefulness of natural processes, and the boundaries of human intervention in nature. Its principles guide us toward a moral evaluation that considers not only the potential benefits of genetic technologies but also their implications for the fundamental nature and purpose of human life.

Moreover, the natural law perspective emphasizes the importance of justice and the common good. It challenges us to consider how genetic technologies impact the most vulnerable among us and the broader human community. Issues of accessibility, equity, and the potential for creating new forms of social and genetic inequality are of paramount concern when evaluating these technologies through the lens of natural law.

In applying natural law to ethical decision-making in the realm of genetic engineering, it is crucial to engage in a reasoned and open-ended inquiry. This process involves assessing the empirical facts of genetic technologies, discerning their moral implications based on the principles of natural law, and considering the consequences of their use for individuals and society.

While natural law offers a robust framework for ethical analysis, it also requires a dialogical approach that acknowledges the complexities of modern science and the plurality of moral perspectives in our global community. Engaging with other ethical theories and the lived experiences of individuals affected by genetic technologies enriches our understanding and application of natural law.

In conclusion, the role of natural law in ethical decision-making on genetic engineering is both significant and complex. It grounds our moral deliberations in the inherent dignity of human life, the teleological order of nature, and the pursuit of the common good. As we navigate the moral terrain of genetic engineering, natural law serves as a vital compass, guiding our efforts to uphold the sanctity of life and the integrity of the natural world.

As the debate over genetic technologies continues to evolve, natural law remains a timeless and critical voice in the conversation. Its principles challenge us to reflect deeply on the moral dimensions of our scientific endeavors and to pursue advancements that honor the dignity of human life and the natural order.

Through a careful and principled application of natural law ethics, we can navigate the ethical challenges of genetic engineering with wisdom and moral integrity. This endeavor requires not only intellectual rigor but also a deep commitment to the values that define us as human beings and guide us in our stewardship of the natural world.

The Principle of Double Effect

The ethical challenges presented by contemporary genetic technologies compel us to revisit age-old moral principles that can guide us through these novel dilemmas. Among these, the Principle of Double Effect stands as a beacon of moral reasoning, shedding light on the complex situations where an action can lead to both good and harmful outcomes. This principle, deeply embedded in the fabric of Catholic ethical thought, resonates with profound implications for genetic editing, gametogenesis, and in vitro fertilization.

At its core, the Principle of Double Effect recognizes that ethical actions can produce two effects: one intended and beneficial, and the other unintended and possibly harmful. Its moral legitimacy hinges on fulfilling four crucial conditions: the action itself must be morally good or neutral; the good effect must not be achieved through the means of the evil effect; the intention must be directed solely towards the good effect, with the evil effect being permitted or tolerated but never desired; and, a proportional reason must exist for allowing the evil effect to occur, weighing the importance of the good effect against the severity of the evil effect.

In the context of genetic editing via CRISPR-Cas9 technology, the Principle of Double Effect offers a nuanced perspective. For instance, editing genes to cure genetic diseases could manifest as the good effect, while potential off-target mutations could represent the unintended harmful effect. Here, the moral evaluation hinges on the intent to cure, the non-exploitative method of achieving this cure, and a proportionate reason—significant health benefits that outweigh the risks of potential harm.

Similarly, this principle can be applied to the ethical evaluation of gametogenesis and in vitro fertilization. These reproductive technologies, while aiming to fulfill the intrinsic human desire for procreation and alleviating the suffering of infertility, introduce ethical conundrums, particularly concerning the dignity and respect for early human life. The Principle of Double Effect necessitates a careful assessment of whether these technologies, in their application, respect the moral law, and whether they represent a proportionate response to the problem of infertility.

However, application of this principle is not without its challenges. The determination of proportionality and the clarity of intention require deep reflection and discernment. Ethical decision-making in the realm of genetics often involves navigating uncertain outcomes and weighing diverse goods and harms in a rapidly evolving scientific landscape. The Principle of Double Effect can serve as a guide, but it necessitates a comprehensive understanding of both the scientific aspects and moral considerations at play.

Moreover, the principle demands a reflection on the societal implications of genetic technologies. The pursuit of genetic editing, for example, must be examined not only in light of individual benefits and harms but also considering its impact on broader social and ethical norms, including issues of justice, equity, and the common good. Here, the Principle of Double Effect reminds us that our ethical considerations must transcend individual cases and address the collective ramifications of our choices.

In the dialogue between Catholic ethics and genetic technology, the Principle of Double Effect stands as a critical tool for moral analysis. It compels us to ask not just about the possible, but about the permissible; it challenges us to consider not only the advancement of science but the advancement of human dignity and ethical integrity. In embracing this principle, ethicists, scientists, and policymakers are invited to a deeper contemplation of the moral landscape, ensuring that our technological capabilities are matched by our ethical wisdom.

It is paramount, therefore, that those involved in the development and application of genetic technologies engage with the Principle of Double Effect with both rigor and humility. This requires an ongoing dialogue between the scientific community and ethicists to ensure that ethical frameworks keep pace with technological advancements. The integration of ethical principles into scientific research and clinical practice is vital for navigating the moral complexities of our genetic future.

As we stand on the brink of unprecedented possibilities in genetic technologies, the Principle of Double Effect offers a lens through which we can evaluate the moral ramifications of our actions. It provides a framework for discerning ethical paths when faced with the dual nature of our choices—reminding us that within the fabric of our decisions lies the potential for both great good and significant harm.

In conclusion, the application of the Principle of Double Effect within the realm of genetic technologies encapsulates the profound ethical challenges of our time. It calls for a delicate balance between scientific innovation and moral responsibility, urging us to tread thoughtfully in our quest to address the maladies that afflict humanity. As we navigate the complexities of genetic engineering, in vitro fertilization, and other biotechnologies, this principle serves as an indispensable tool in our ethical arsenal, guiding us towards choices that uphold the dignity of human life and the principles of Catholic moral teaching.

Chapter 2: Understanding Genetic Engineering

The exploration of genetic engineering involves navigating a labyrinth of scientific innovation, each turn revealing new ethical, theological, and philosophical considerations. This chapter aims to dissect the intricate world of genetic modification, its mechanisms, its history, and the ongoing dialogue within ethical frameworks, particularly through a Catholic lens.

At the heart of genetic engineering is the ability to manipulate the genetic makeup of organisms, including humans, with precision previously thought unattainable. This manipulation hinges on technologies like CRISPR-Cas9, a tool that has revolutionized the field by allowing for the editing of DNA sequences and the regulation of gene activity. Such capabilities raise profound questions about the ontological status of genetically modified organisms and the potential to alter what it means to be human fundamentally.

Historically, the journey through genetic research has been marked by both remarkable discoveries and ethical dilemmas. Starting with Mendel's early work on heredity in pea plants, moving through the discovery of DNA's double helix structure by Watson and Crick, to the advent of the Human Genome Project, each milestone has expanded our understanding of biology while challenging our moral compasses. Today's advancements, particularly around CRISPR, represent not merely another step but a giant leap in that ongoing journey.

The philosophical implications of these technologies are as vast as they are complex. For one, the ability to edit genes presents a paradigm shift from accepting the natural order to asserting control over it. This shift invites a reevaluation of natural law, a cornerstone of Catholic ethical teaching, and prompts a discussion on the balance between human ingenuity and humility before nature's given order.

The ethical discourse surrounding genetic engineering often oscillates between the potential for profound benefits and the risk of significant harm. On one hand, genetic modification holds the promise of eradicating hereditary diseases, improving agricultural yields, and pushing the boundaries of scientific knowledge. On the other, it brings forward the specter of eugenics, the commodification of life, and the possibility of irreversible harm to the genetic fabric of the natural world.

In considering these ethical quandaries, it becomes essential to anchor deliberations in the dignity of human life. This principle, deeply embedded in Catholic thought, serves as a critical lens through which the moral dimensions of genetic engineering are examined. It champions the view that any genetic manipulation must be geared towards the genuine good of the person and the broader creation, safeguarding against ventures into genetic enhancement driven by vanity or profit.

The narrative of genetic engineering is replete with moral lessons and theological insights. It serves as a contemporary arena where timeless ethical questions emerge with new urgency. The Catholic intellectual tradition, with its emphasis on the sanctity of life, the common good, and the moral law, provides a rich framework for engaging with these questions. It encourages a holistic view that considers not only the technical aspects of genetic manipulation but also its spiritual, societal, and ecological implications.

As we move forward into the uncharted territories of genetic innovation, the moral compass provided by Catholic ethics can help guide scientific exploration towards the true good of humanity and the whole creation. This journey requires not only a deep understanding of the science behind genetic technologies but also a critical engagement with the ethical, philosophical, and theological dimensions that these technologies entail.

In essence, understanding genetic engineering is not just about comprehending its mechanisms but also about grappling with the profound ethical questions it poses. It is about recognizing the immense power entailed in rewriting the code of life and confronting the responsibilities that come with wielding such power. As we advance further into the genetic frontier, it is imperative that our scientific ambitions are matched by an equally vigorous ethical inquiry.

Conclusively, while the future of genetic engineering is fraught with uncertainties, it also presents an opportunity for humanity to reflect on its values, aspirations, and limitations. By engaging in a thoughtful and informed dialogue, grounded in enduring ethical principles, we can hope to navigate the complexities of genetic engineering in a manner that honors the dignity of all life.

The Science Behind Genetic Editing Technologies

The journey into the crux of genetic editing technologies unveils a landscape where science and ethics intersect, marked by advancements and ethical conundrums. This exploration delves deep into the mechanics and implications of manipulating the very code that defines living organisms. Genetic editing, at its core, involves the precision alteration of DNA sequences within the genome of an organism. It's a field that has witnessed significant strides, notably through technologies such as CRISPR-Cas9, which have propelled our capabilities into a new era of genetic engineering.

At the heart of genetic editing lies DNA, the molecule that carries the genetic instructions used in the growth, development, functioning, and reproduction of all known living organisms and many viruses. DNA is composed of two strands that wind around each other to form a double helix, comprising sequences of nucleotides that encode the genetic information. Genetic editing technologies manipulate these sequences, correcting mutations, introducing beneficial modifications, or studying the function of genes.

CRISPR-Cas9 has emerged as a groundbreaking tool in this field, offering unprecedented precision, efficiency, and flexibility in editing the DNA of organisms. Originally discovered as a part of the bacterial immune system, CRISPR-Cas9 can precisely target and cut DNA at desired locations, allowing for the removal, addition, or alteration of specific genetic sequences. This process, akin to cutting and pasting text in a word processor, has not only revolutionized basic research but also opened new doors for the treatment of genetic disorders, agricultural enhancements, and even the potential eradication of diseases.

However, the advent of genetic editing technologies brings forth a profound ethical quandary. As we tread further into the fabric of life, altering genetic material raises questions about the essence of nature and the boundaries of human intervention. It beckons us to ponder upon the sanctity of life and the implications of our newfound capacities to edit the book of life.

One cannot ignore the potential benefits genetic editing technologies herald for medicine and agriculture. The promise of curing genetic diseases, improving crop resilience, and combating pathogens offers a glimpse into a future where the quality of life is significantly enhanced. Yet, these potential advancements are not without their moral and ethical complications.

The alteration of the human germline — that is, making changes to the genetic code that can be inherited by future generations — presents a particularly contentious ethical frontier. It raises profound questions about consent, the nature of humanity, and the potential for unforeseen consequences. The ramifications of such alterations extend far beyond the individual, touching upon the genetic heritage of the human species.

Moreover, the accessibility of genetic editing technologies underscores issues of inequality and justice. The prospect of life-enhancing genetic modifications being available only to those who can afford them exacerbates existing disparities, potentially leading to a new form of genetic class divide. It is imperative to consider how these technologies can be ethically harnessed while ensuring equitable access.

The Catholic ethic, with its emphasis on the dignity of human life, natural law, and the common good, offers a critical lens through which to examine the moral dimensions of genetic editing. In navigating these waters, one must weigh the potential for alleviating suffering against the imperative to respect the natural order and the sanctity of the human person.

As we venture deeper into the capabilities of genetic engineering, it becomes increasingly important to engage in a multidisciplinary dialogue involving scientists, ethicists, theologians, and policymakers. This conversation must strive to balance the pursuit of knowledge and the betterment of humanity with the moral principles that guide us.

Furthermore, the environmental implications of genetic editing technologies cannot be overlooked. The modification of organisms could have unforeseen effects on ecosystems and biodiversity. It necessitates a careful and considered approach that respects the interconnectedness of all creation.

In grappling with the ethical considerations of genetic editing, we are reminded of the complexity and responsibility that accompany our scientific endeavors. The potential to do good is vast, yet so is the potential to alter the course of life in irreversible ways.

It is, therefore, incumbent upon us to approach genetic editing technologies with a sense of humility and a deep commitment to ethical stewardship. As we push the boundaries of what is scientifically possible, we must also safeguard the moral and ethical boundaries that define our humanity.

In conclusion, the science behind genetic editing technologies represents a pivotal chapter in the unfolding story of human progress. As we decode the mysteries of life, we are confronted with profound ethical questions that challenge us to reflect on what it means to be human. The path forward requires a careful balancing of the promise and perils that accompany these technologies, guided by a moral compass that ensures the dignity and welfare of all life.

Historical Milestones in Genetic Research

The journey through the annals of genetic research unveils a tapestry rich with intellectual rigor, ethical quandaries, and momentous discoveries that have irrevocably shaped our understanding of life itself. This narrative began in earnest with the pioneering work of Gregor Mendel in the 19th century. Mendel's meticulous experimentation with pea plants laid the foundational principles of inheritance, introducing the world to the concepts of dominant and recessive genes. Though Mendel's contributions were not fully appreciated until years after his death, his work marked the inception of genetic science (Henig, 2000).

The 20th century heralded a rapid acceleration in genetic research, culminating in the elucidation of the DNA's double helix structure by James Watson and Francis Crick in 1953, a discovery that unlocked the molecular basis of inheritance. This pivotal moment, built upon the foundational work of Rosalind Franklin and Maurice Wilkins, who played critical roles in understanding the physical structure of DNA, set the stage for the modern era of genetic engineering (Watson, 1968). Advances in molecular biology techniques thereafter, including the development of recombinant DNA technology in the 1970s, enabled scientists to manipulate genetic material in ways previously unimaginable, ushering in new possibilities for medicine, agriculture, and biotechnology (Ijaz & Haq, 2020).

The advent of CRISPR-Cas9 technology in the 21st century represents the latest frontier in the saga of genetic research, offering unprecedented precision in gene editing. This technology has not only galvanized the scientific community but has also ignited a robust debate among ethicists, theologians, and the wider public about the moral implications of gene editing. As we stand on the precipice of a future where the boundaries of genetic intervention are continually expanding, it becomes imperative to engage with these technologies through a lens that encompasses not only the scientific and technical considerations but also the profound ethical and moral dimensions (Doudna & Charpentier, 2016).

From Mendel to CRISPR: A Journey Through Time

The chronicle of genetic science isn't just a tale of scientific endeavor; it's a profound narrative interwoven with the complexities of human curiosity, ethical quandaries, and the boundless quest for understanding life itself. A pivotal figure in this journey was Gregor Mendel, whose meticulous cross-breeding experiments with pea plants in the mid-19th century laid the foundational principles of heredity and genetics. Mendel's work, unappreciated in his own time, eventually became the cornerstone upon which modern genetics would be built.

However, the road from Mendel's pea garden to the sophisticated gene-editing capabilities of CRISPR has been anything but direct. For decades, Mendel's discoveries remained a curious footnote in the annals of biology, overshadowed by the burgeoning fields of Darwinian evolution and cytology. It wasn't until the early 20th century that the significance of Mendel's work was rediscovered, catalyzing a revolution in the understanding of inheritance, evolution, and cell biology.

The synthesis of Mendelian genetics with Darwinian evolution in the form of the Modern Synthesis in the mid-20th century further refined our understanding of genetic principles. This era of discovery paved the way for the identification and understanding of DNA as the molecule carrying genetic information, thanks to the pivotal work of James Watson, Francis Crick, Rosalind Franklin, and others in the 1950s. Their research elucidated the double helix structure of DNA, setting the stage for the ensuing genetic revolution.

The latter half of the 20th century witnessed burgeoning advancements in genetic engineering, including the development of recombinant DNA technology. This allowed for the insertion of DNA from one organism into another, a groundbreaking advance with profound implications for medicine, agriculture, and industry. Yet, with these capabilities came ethical dilemmas, sparking debates that would only intensify with time.

The advent of the Human Genome Project in the late 20th century marked a bold effort to map all the genes in the human genome. Completed in 2003, this project not only advanced our understanding of genetic predisposition to diseases but also raised questions about privacy, discrimination, and the nature of human identity.

Enter CRISPR-Cas9, a gene-editing tool derived from a bacterial immune defense system, which has dramatically transformed genetic engineering's landscape. Discovered by Jennifer Doudna and Emmanuelle Charpentier, CRISPR technology allows for precise, targeted changes to the DNA of plants, animals, and humans, heralding an era of unprecedented genetic manipulation capabilities.

The scientific potential of CRISPR technology is immense, offering the promise of curing genetic diseases, improving crop resilience, and even eradicating vectors of devastating illnesses like malaria. Yet, its capacity for irreversible alterations to the genome introduces profound ethical concerns, particularly within the context of human germline editing. The prospect of designer babies, the implications for human evolution, and the accessibility of such technology across different socio-economic groups are subjects of intense debate within the scientific community and beyond.

For the Roman Catholic Church and Catholic ethicists, the advent of CRISPR emphasizes the necessity of a moral framework grounded in the sanctity of human life and the dignity of the human person. The potential for gene editing to cure diseases aligns with the Church's mission to heal and care for the sick; however, the possibility of altering the human germline or creating genetically modified humans raises profound concerns about the manipulation of creation and the essence of what it means to be human.

The Church's engagement with these issues is nuanced, advocating for scientific advancement that respects human dignity and the natural law, while cautioning against practices that commodify human life or erode the fundamental values of human society. The unique capabilities of CRISPR, thus, represent not merely a scientific milestone but a crossroads at which ethical, theological, and philosophical questions converge.

As we advance from Mendel's garden to the forefront of genetic editing, the journey through time is marked by incredible scientific achievements, each accompanied by its own set of ethical considerations. The Catholic Church, with its rich tradition of engaging with scientific inquiry within an ethical and moral framework, continues to play a pivotal role in navigating these new frontiers.

The dialogue between science and faith, particularly in the domain of genetic engineering, is not a confrontation but a necessary partnership. It seeks to harness the undeniable potential of technologies like CRISPR for the betterment of humanity while steadfastly upholding the principles of human dignity and ethical integrity.

In summary, the journey from Mendel to CRISPR is not just a chronicle of biological discovery but a testament to the human desire to understand, improve, and, at times, control the essence of life itself. It underscores the significant responsibility that comes with such power—the duty to ensure that our scientific capabilities are matched by our ethical wisdom and respect for the sanctity of life.

Chapter 3: CRISPR and Catholic Bioethics

The debate surrounding CRISPR-Cas9 technology and its ethical implications within Catholic bioethics exemplifies the challenging intersection between groundbreaking scientific discoveries and the enduring moral principles of the Church. At the heart of Catholic bioethics is the unwavering commitment to the dignity of human life, a principle that inevitably comes under scrutiny with the advent of technologies capable of altering the human genome at its most fundamental level.

CRISPR-Cas9, a revolutionary genetic editing tool, offers unprecedented opportunities for the treatment of genetic disorders, potentially eradicating diseases like sickle cell anemia and cystic fibrosis. However, alongside these promising applications are ethical quandaries that challenge Catholic moral teaching. The manipulation of the human germline—changes that would be passed down to future generations—raises significant concerns about playing God, the sanctity of human creation, and the potential for unforeseen consequences spanning generations. The Church's engagement with these issues underscores a delicate balance: recognizing the potential for alleviating human suffering while safeguarding the intrinsic value of human life at every stage of development and in every form it takes.

An ethical assessment of CRISPR within the Catholic tradition cannot be divorced from the principle of natural law, which posits that moral goodness is determined by the degree to which an action corresponds with the natural order intended by God. This outlook poses critical questions about human intervention in the genetic code, a fundamental element of the natural order. While therapeutic endeavors aimed at curing disease align with the Christian duty to alleviate suffering, enhancements or modifications for non-therapeutic purposes venture into murky ethical waters, potentially conflicting with the Creator's design and human integrity as created in the image of God.

Moreover, the principle of double effect, another pillar of Catholic ethical reasoning, provides a framework for evaluating situations where a morally permissible act may have both positive and negative consequences. Applying this principle to CRISPR, the Church might support genetic editing with the primary intention of curing a genetic disorder, even if it carries potential unintended negative effects, provided that the good effect is not achieved through wrong means and the potential harm is not disproportionate.

The dialogue between the Church and the scientific community on the ethical use of CRISPR technology is emblematic of a broader challenge: navigating the frontiers of biotechnology while adhering to timeless moral principles. As CRISPR-Cas9 technology progresses, the Church's bioethical framework offers an invaluable lens through which to evaluate the moral dimensions of genetic editing, emphasizing both the promise it holds and the perils it poses. This delicate negotiation between hope for medical advances and the imperative to protect human dignity underscores the profound implications of these technologies for humanity's understanding of itself and its stewardship of creation.

An Overview of CRISPR-Cas9 Technology

Clustered Regularly Interspaced Short Palindromic Repeats (CRISPR) and CRISPR-associated protein 9 (Cas9) technology have revolutionized the field of genetic engineering. This technology allows for precise, targeted changes to an organism's DNA, offering unprecedented potential for advancements in medicine, agriculture, and beyond. At its core, CRISPR-Cas9 functions as a form of molecular scissors, capable of cutting DNA strands at specific locations. This enables the removal, addition, or alteration of sections of the DNA sequence.

The CRISPR-Cas9 system was inspired by a natural defense mechanism found in bacteria. These microorganisms use CRISPR sequences as a form of immunological memory to recognize and destroy viral genetic material. Scientists Jennifer Doudna and Emmanuelle Charpentier were pivotal in adapting this bacterial system for use in genetic engineering, laying the groundwork for the CRISPR-Cas9 technology that we are familiar with today (Doudna & Charpentier, 2016).

The applications of CRISPR-Cas9 are vast and varied. In medicine, it holds the promise of curing genetic diseases by correcting mutations at their source. For agriculture, it offers the potential to engineer crops that are more nutritious, resilient to climate change, and capable of yielding larger harvests. Nonetheless, while the breadth of its applications is thrilling, it ushers in a host of ethical considerations.

One of the most pressing ethical concerns surrounds the use of CRISPR-Cas9 in human embryos. The prospect of germline editing raises the possibility of eradicating inheritable diseases, but it also poses significant ethical dilemmas around the nature of consent, the potential for unforeseen consequences in the genetic makeup of individuals, and the specter of eugenics. The Catholic Church, alongside various ethical bodies, has voiced concerns about the sanctity of life and the moral implications of altering the human germline.

In the context of agriculture, CRISPR technology's promise to revolutionize food production must be weighed against concerns about biodiversity, ecological impact, and the ethics of patenting genetically edited organisms. The

Catholic tradition's emphasis on stewardship of creation provides a unique lens through which to examine these issues, advocating for an approach that respects the integrity of creation while recognizing humanity's role in its preservation and enhancement.

Moreover, the development and deployment of CRISPR-Cas9 technology prompt a discussion about accessibility and equity. The potential to alleviate human suffering through genetic therapies is tremendous, yet this raises questions about who will have access to these advances. The Catholic social teaching principle of the preferential option for the poor mandates that the benefits of genetic engineering must be accessible to all, particularly the most vulnerable, rather than exclusively to those who can afford them.

The promise of CRISPR also extends to the realm of environmental conservation. By potentially enabling the engineering of species to combat invasive species or diseases decimating wildlife populations, CRISPR could play a role in preserving biodiversity. However, this application again requires careful ethical scrutiny, balancing the potential benefits against risks of unforeseen consequences on ecosystems.

CRISPR-Cas9 technology, with its ability to edit genes with precision, also ignites debates about the definition of what it means to be human. The possibility of not just treating genetic diseases but enhancing human capacities (so-called "designer babies") challenges traditional understandings of human nature and dignity. The Catholic perspective, which views human beings as created in the image of God and endowed with inherent dignity, provides critical insight into these discussions.

In summary, while CRISPR-Cas9 technology harbors great promise for advancing human health, agricultural productivity, and ecological conservation, it also raises profound ethical questions. These include considerations around the sanctity of human life, the integrity of creation, social justice, and the very nature of human identity and dignity. Addressing these concerns requires a careful balance between harnessing the potential benefits of CRISPR technology and upholding moral principles that respect life and creation.

As we stand on the precipice of a new era in genetic engineering, it is imperative for the Catholic community, ethicists, and society at large to engage in thoughtful dialogue. This dialogue must navigate the complex moral landscape presented by CRISPR-Cas9 technology, striving to promote the common good while safeguarding against potential misuse and harm. The goal is not to retreat from the frontiers of science, but to advance with ethical integrity, respecting the dignity of life in all its forms.

Through engagement with these ethical considerations, we can hope to harness the potential of CRISPR-Cas9 technology in a manner that aligns with the highest aspirations of humanity. This journey requires not only scientific insight but also moral wisdom, calling us to tread carefully as we shape the genetic foundations of the future.

The Promise and Perils of CRISPR

The discovery and integration of CRISPR-Cas9 technology constitute a significant milestone in the annals of scientific innovation, offering unparalleled precision in the domain of genetic engineering. Its promises are vast, including the potential eradication of hereditary diseases, the enhancement of crop resilience, and even the possibility of curtailing the spread of vector-borne diseases such as malaria. Yet, the enthusiasm for these advancements is met with an equally weighted apprehension within the Catholic bioethical framework, which emphasizes the sanctity of life, the natural order, and the intrinsic dignity of the human person. Herein, we delve into the nuanced interplay between the optimistic potential and the ethical quandaries posed by CRISPR within this context.

On the one hand, CRISPR's promise of alleviating human suffering aligns with the compassionate outreach inherent in Catholic social teaching. The possibility of correcting genetic anomalies that cause debilitating conditions such as cystic fibrosis, Huntington's disease, and sickle cell anemia presents a compelling narrative of healing and relief from suffering. This aspect of CRISPR embodies an expression of care and solidarity with those burdened by the maladies of our fallen nature, showcasing the potential for science and faith to coalesce in the alleviation of human suffering.

However, the perils of CRISPR technology resonate profoundly with concerns over human dignity and the integrity of creation. The prospect of germline editing, which entails modifications not just to the individual but to their progeny, thrusts us into uncharted ethical territories. It begets questions about the essence of human nature and the boundaries of human intervention in creation. From a Catholic perspective, such interventions must be cautiously scrutinized for their implications on the sanctity of life and the potential commodification of human existence. There is a palpable concern that the pursuit of genetic perfection could eclipse the inherent worth of every life, regardless of its physical or genetic conditions.

A significant peril of CRISPR technology lies in its potential for misuse under the guise of enhancement or perfection. The differentiation between therapeutic uses aimed at addressing specific diseases and enhancements aimed at augmenting human capabilities is a blurred line fraught with ethical dilemmas. The prospect of 'designer babies,' characterized by selected genetic traits, raises profound questions about equality, diversity, and the essence of human identity.

Another concern centers on the environmental and societal implications of broad CRISPR applications. Gene drives, designed to propagate specific genetic traits rapidly within a population, could theoretically mitigate diseases spread by insects or bolster agricultural yields. However, the long-term ecological impacts remain uncertain, and the potential for unforeseen consequences is a source of ethical consternation. The principle of prudence, deeply ingrained in Catholic teaching, calls for a cautious approach to technologies that could irrevocably alter the natural world.

The ethical landscape of CRISPR is further complicated by issues of justice and accessibility. The potential for disparities in access to genetic therapies could exacerbate existing inequalities, leading to a bifurcation of society into genetic 'haves' and 'have-nots.' This scenario is antithetical to the Catholic emphasis on the common good and the preferential option for the poor, raising alarms about the equitable distribution of the fruits of genetic innovations.

In light of these considerations, the Catholic response to CRISPR is not one of outright rejection but of critical, ethical discernment. It necessitates a vigilant examination of both the intent and the consequences of genetic editing within the framework of moral principles that prioritize the dignity of life, the stewardship of creation, and the common good. This approach is emblematic of the Church's endeavor to engage with the modern world, affirming the positive potential of scientific advancements while steadfastly advocating for their responsible and ethical use.

Within this dialectic of promise and peril, the Catholic ethical tradition offers a compass for navigating the moral quandaries posed by CRISPR. It provides a nuanced perspective that appreciates the potential benefits of genetic engineering while vigilantly guarding against its ethical pitfalls. As humanity stands on the cusp of this genetic frontier, the wisdom of Catholic bioethics can illuminate a path that cherishes the gift of life and safeguards the integrity of creation.

Therefore, as we consider the future of CRISPR and its integration into medical practice and societal development, we are called to a dialogue that transcends scientific and technological achievements. It is a conversation deeply entrenched in the values we hold dear, reflecting our profoundest beliefs about the nature of human dignity, the sanctity of life, and the moral fabric of our society. In this dialogue, Catholic bioethics provides a critical voice, reminding us that at the heart of every technological advancement lie questions of profound moral significance, demanding our vigilant attention and thoughtful response.

In conclusion, while CRISPR technology beckons with promises of a brighter, healthier future, it also presents perils that require careful ethical consideration. The Catholic Church, with its rich tradition of moral reflection, offers valuable insights into the discernment process, advocating for a balanced approach that embraces the potential for good while guarding against the dangers of overreach and ethical lapses. As we forge ahead into this new genetic era, it is incumbent upon us to heed these insights, ensuring that our advancements in genetic engineering serve the welfare of all humanity and the greater glory of creation.

Ethical Considerations and Church Teaching As we delve deeper into the implications of CRISPR technology, it is imperative to juxtapose the scientific potential with the ethical teachings and principles upheld by the Catholic Church. In this intricate dance between advancement and morality, the Church's guidance offers a beacon of light that aims to navigate the complexities of genetic manipulation within the sanctity of human life.

The Catholic Church has long been a proponent of scientific discovery, advocating for the advancement of knowledge that upholds the dignity of humanity and the care of creation. However, this support comes with meticulous ethical scrutiny, particularly when the technology possesses the power to alter the very essence of human life. CRISPR, for all its promise, presents such a challenge—a potent tool capable of great good yet fraught with moral peril.

At the heart of the Church's ethical considerations is the belief in the inherent dignity of every human being, created in the image and likeness of God. This foundational principle demands respect for human life from conception to natural end, guiding the Church's stance on various bioethical issues, including genetic editing.

The Church acknowledges the potential of CRISPR and similar technologies to heal and prevent diseases, a pursuit deeply aligned with the Christian commitment to alleviate human suffering. Nevertheless, the application of such technologies raises critical ethical questions, particularly when it comes to modifying the germ line—changes that would not only affect the individual but also be passed down to future generations, potentially altering the course of human evolution.

An ethical analysis of CRISPR within the Church's teaching framework cannot disregard the principle of double effect, which evaluates the permissibility of an action that causes a serious harm as a side effect of promoting some good end. The manipulation of genes, even with noble intentions such as the eradication of hereditary diseases, must be scrutinized for its unintended consequences, which may include unforeseen health issues and socio-ethical implications that span beyond individual patients to society at large.

The natural law, another cornerstone of Catholic moral teaching, offers insights into the ethical evaluation of genetic engineering. This principle advocates for actions that align with the natural order and purpose of things as created by God. From this perspective, interventions that aim to correct genetic defects may be ethically justifiable, provided they respect the integrity of the person and do not usurp the Creator's role or demean human dignity.

However, the Church vehemently opposes the use of genetic editing for non-therapeutic purposes, such as the creation of so-called "designer babies." Such practices not only breach the ethical norms concerning the sanctity of life and the natural order but also raise grave concerns about inequality, discrimination, and the commodification of human life. The pursuit of a perceived genetic perfection can lead to a slippery slope, marginalizing those with disabilities and promoting a culture of eugenics.

The concept of stewardship, deeply embedded in Catholic teaching, further informs the ethical debate on genetic editing. Humans are called to be caretakers of God's creation, a responsibility that encompasses respect for the genetic integrity of species. While genetic manipulation for purposes such as crop improvement could be considered within the bounds of responsible stewardship, these actions must be weighed against potential risks to human health and environmental balance.

In evaluating the ethical implications of CRISPR, the Church emphasizes the importance of intention and context. Genetic editing aimed at treating or preventing diseases could be morally acceptable if conducted within an ethical framework that respects human dignity, adheres to the principle of do no harm, and is motivated by genuine humanitarian concern rather than profit or prestige.

Another concern is the accessibility of these technologies. The Catholic Church's preferential option for the poor mandates special attention to the most vulnerable members of society. Technology that holds the promise of curing diseases must be accessible to all, not just the wealthy or those living in developed countries. This principle challenges the global community to seek equitable solutions that bridge the gap between technological possibility and accessibility.

Consent and autonomy also play crucial roles in the ethical evaluation of CRISPR use, particularly within the context of Catholic teaching. Individuals must have the autonomy to make informed decisions regarding their own genetic makeup and that of their offspring. Yet, this autonomy exists within the bounds of moral order and must be guided by an informed conscience that seeks the greater good.

Dialogue and collaboration between the scientific community and ethical, religious, and societal leaders are essential to navigate the moral landscape shaped by CRISPR and other genetic technologies. The Church advocates for a collective discernment process that respects diverse viewpoints while grounding decisions in ethical principles that promote human dignity and the common good.

In conclusion, the Catholic Church's teaching provides a comprehensive moral framework for evaluating CRISPR technology, emphasizing the need for ethical discernment that upholds human dignity, respects the natural order, and promotes the common good. As humanity stands on the brink of potentially revolutionary genetic breakthroughs, the Church's teachings offer vital ethical guidelines that foster a just and compassionate application of these technologies.

Case Studies: Gene Editing in Humans In the ongoing dialogue between science and religion, particularly within the context of Catholic bioethics, the exploration of gene editing in humans holds a place of complex intrigue. Drawing from a diversity of sources, this section engages with case studies that illuminate the ethical quandaries inherent in the application of CRISPR-Cas9 technology on human subjects. These cases have been selected for their salience to the moral, philosophical, and theological considerations that shape Catholic bioethical perspectives.

The emergence of CRISPR-Cas9 as a precise tool for genetic modification has brought to the forefront the potential to address genetic disorders at their source. Scientists, equipped with this technology, have stepped into the realm of editing human genes, both somatic and germline, with the aim of curing inherited diseases. Each case study presented here invites an examination of the moral implications, weighing the potential benefits against the ethical concerns laid out by Catholic teaching.

One such case involves the use of CRISPR to correct a gene responsible for sickle cell disease, a debilitating condition that affects millions worldwide. Somatic gene editing, in this instance, targets the cells of an individual patient, with no implications for hereditary transmission. From a Catholic ethical standpoint, this application raises questions about the sanctity of life, the natural law, and the potential for unintentional consequences, despite its therapeutic intentions.

Another case examines the experiment conducted in China by scientist He Jiankui, who utilized CRISPR technology to edit the genes of twin girls with the intention of making them resistant to HIV. This case steps into the more controversial terrain of germline editing, whereby genetic changes can be inherited by future generations. The ethical implications of this act, including concerns about consent, the sanctity of human life, and the potential for unforeseeable alterations to human nature, have elicited widespread debate within both scientific and Catholic ethical circles.

Additional cases of gene editing in humans highlight the ongoing efforts to combat genetically linked diseases such as Huntington's disease and cystic fibrosis. These conditions, deeply ingrained in the genetic code of individuals, present significant moral dilemmas when considering gene editing as a form of treatment. The application of CRISPR technology, in these cases, forces a reflection on the principles of Catholic teaching, particularly the concepts of human dignity, the common good, and the precautionary principle.

Each case study, with its specific focus and outcomes, serves as a focal point for discussing the ethical considerations of intervening in the human genome. The Catholic Church, emphasizing the inherent dignity of every human life and the importance of natural law, provides a framework for evaluating these technological advances. While recognizing the potential for significant therapeutic benefits, the Church also calls for a cautious approach that respects the integrity of creation and the rights of all individuals.

The exploration of gene editing in humans, especially through the lens of individual case studies, reveals a tension between the desire to alleviate human suffering and the imperative to uphold ethical standards. This tension, central to the discourse on genetic engineering within Catholic bioethics, necessitates a nuanced understanding of both the scientific and moral dimensions of gene editing technologies.

Through the examination of these case studies, it becomes apparent that the ethical landscape of gene editing is fraught with complexities. Each instance of gene editing, whether for therapeutic or experimental purposes, must be carefully evaluated in light of Catholic moral principles. This includes considerations of the potential for harm, the respect for autonomy and informed consent, and the implications of altering the human genetic heritage.

Moreover, the discussion of gene editing in humans raises important questions about social justice and equity. The availability of genetic therapies, the potential for their misuse, and the risk of exacerbating existing inequalities present significant ethical challenges that must be addressed within the framework of Catholic social teaching.

The debate on gene editing also touches on the concept of human enhancement. The distinction between therapeutic interventions and enhancements intended to surpass the typical human capacities is a subject of ethical scrutiny.

Catholic bioethics, with its emphasis on the dignity of the human person and the natural order, offers critical insights into the discussion of enhancement versus therapy.

In conclusion, the case studies of gene editing in humans presented here underscore the richness and complexity of the ethical discourse within Catholic bioethics. By engaging with specific instances of CRISPR-Cas9 application in human subjects, this discourse contributes to a broader understanding of the moral and philosophical implications of genetic engineering. In navigating this terrain, it is paramount to hold in balance the potential benefits of genetic therapies with the enduring values of human dignity, natural law, and ethical integrity.

The Church's Stance on Gametogenesis

In examining the Church's position regarding gametogenesis, we explore a domain where science and divine teaching intersect, offering a profound reflection on the principles of life's sacred beginning. Gametogenesis, the process by which gametes are produced for sexual reproduction, has opened up new frontiers in reproductive technology, including the potential for creating life outside the conventional paradigms of human procreation. Within this context, the Church's perspective is both critical and instructive, providing guidance that navigates the intricate balance between the marvels of scientific achievement and the moral imperatives that ground human dignity and life's sanctity.

The emergence of technologies enabling artificial gametogenesis raises ethical quandaries that challenge traditional Catholic teachings on procreation, parenthood, and the natural order. The Church, guided by centuries-old doctrine and a commitment to the inviolability of life from conception, scrutinizes these developments through the lens of its moral principles, notably those articulated in the natural law tradition. This tradition posits that moral reasoning is rooted in understanding the natural purposes and ends of human faculties and actions. Thus, interventions like artificial gametogenesis are evaluated regarding their consonance with the natural ends of human reproduction and the unitive purpose of marital relations. The creation of human life, in the Church's view, should not be detached from the marital act, which is both unitive and procreative, reflecting the comprehensive dimensions of human love and responsibility (Catechism of the Catholic Church, 1997).

Furthermore, the Church's reflections on gametogenesis extend beyond the process itself to encompass the implications for the resulting human beings. The ethical challenges born from these technologies include concerns about the commodification of human life, the disruption of familial and societal bonds, and the potential inequalities generated by access to such technologies. The concern for the dignity of every human being, central to Catholic social teaching, informs a cautious stance towards any biotechnological advance that could diminish the inherent value of human life or alter its foundational social contexts. As such, the Church advocates for a rigorous ethical scrutiny that places the sanctity and dignity of human life at the forefront of any discussion on artificial gametogenesis, seeking to foster a culture that respects life in all its stages and expressions.

Defining Gametogenesis and Its Applications

Gametogenesis, a critical process in the cycle of life, encompasses the formation and development of the male and female gametes, the sperm, and the ovum, respectively. This complex biological process involves the reduction division, known as meiosis, whereby the chromosome number is halved, ensuring that upon fertilization, the ensuing zygote harbors the species-specific chromosome count. In recent years, advancements in biotechnology have extended the realm of gametogenesis beyond the confines of natural biological functions to encompass in vitro applications, giving rise to a myriad of ethical, moral, and theological considerations, especially within the domain of Catholic bioethics.

The scientific community has made significant strides in unraveling the intricacies of gametogenesis, leading to revolutionary applications such as in vitro gametogenesis (IVG). This technology, though still in its infancy, has the potential to allow for the creation of gametes outside the human body, using cells that are not inherently germ cells. The implications of such capability are vast and varied, ranging from providing solutions for infertility to opening the door to new forms of genetic selection and manipulation.

The application of gametogenesis, particularly through IVG, offers hope to countless individuals and couples grappling with infertility challenges. By unlocking the possibility of creating viable gametes from somatic cells, IVG could potentially enable those who, due to various medical conditions, are unable to conceive naturally, to have genetically related offspring. This aspect of gametogenesis stands as a beacon of hope, illuminating the path towards fulfilling the innate human desire for procreation and lineage continuity.

However, alongside the promise, gametogenesis, especially when executed in vitro, introduces a plethora of ethical considerations. The manipulation of the basic units of human life raises questions regarding the sanctity of life, the natural order, and the moral boundaries of human intervention in the creation of life. The Catholic Church, with its rich tradition of moral theology and bioethics, approaches these questions from the standpoint of fundamental principles such as the dignity of human life, the sanctity of procreation, and the integrity of marriage and family life.

In exploring the applications of gametogenesis, it's crucial to consider the process within the broader theological and ethical framework that governs Catholic teaching on life and procreation. The Church's perspectives on these matters are deeply rooted in the belief in the inherent dignity of every human being, created in the image and likeness of God, and the conviction that the process of bringing new life into the world is sacred and should be aligned with the divine plan for creation.

The potential of gametogenesis to alter the natural course of human reproduction invites a reevaluation of traditional ethical notions concerning the marital act and the transmission of life. In vitro gametogenesis, by enabling the creation of human gametes outside the context of marital union, challenges the Catholic understanding of the procreative purpose of marriage. Such technological advancements compel the Church to articulate responses that reaffirm the intrinsic value of human life and the sanctity of the conjugal act as the natural and moral context for human procreation.

Beyond the realm of human reproduction, the applications of gametogenesis extend to the sphere of genetic research and therapy. The ability to create gametes in vitro offers scientists a valuable tool for studying the complex processes of human development and genetic diseases. This aspect of gametogenesis presents a promising avenue for advancing medical knowledge and developing treatments that could alleviate suffering and enhance the quality of life for individuals afflicted with hereditary conditions.

Nonetheless, the utilization of gametogenesis for purposes of genetic manipulation, including the selection and modification of genetic traits, introduces significant ethical dilemmas. The prospect of 'designer babies,' whose genetic makeup is artificially selected or altered to possess desired traits, raises profound moral questions about the nature of human dignity and the limits of human dominion over creation. The Catholic Church, in its commitment to defending the intrinsic worth of every human life, irrespective of physical or genetic characteristics, stands as a critical voice in the discourse on these emerging biotechnological powers.

Moreover, the advent of gametogenesis technology brings to the forefront concerns regarding justice and access. The potential for such medical interventions to exacerbate existing inequalities, by making cutting-edge reproductive technologies available only to the privileged few, challenges the Church's teachings on the preferential option for the poor and the common good. It is imperative, therefore, to engage in a critical examination of the societal implications of gametogenesis, to ensure that advances in this field serve the welfare of all humanity, rather than widening the chasm between the affluent and the less fortunate.

The dialogue between science and faith, particularly in the realm of gametogenesis, must be approached with humility, openness, and a profound respect for the mystery of life. The Church's contribution to this exchange is invaluable, offering ethical principles and moral guidance grounded in a comprehensive vision of the human person and the common good. In navigating the moral terrain shaped by advancements in gametogenesis, the insights of Catholic bioethics serve as a compass, directing the scientific community and society at large towards a future where the dignity of every human life is upheld and cherished.

As we stand on the threshold of unprecedented technological capabilities in the field of reproductive biology, the Church is called to exercise prudent discernment. This entails a careful consideration of the scientific facts of gametogenesis, the potential applications and implications of this technology, and the ethical principles that must guide our response. In doing so, the Church fulfills its mission to illuminate the path of progress with the light of the Gospel, ensuring that our collective journey towards scientific advancements is marked by a deep respect for the inviolable sanctity of human life.

In conclusion, gametogenesis, with its profound implications for human reproduction, genetic research, and therapy, occupies a critical juncture where science and faith intersect. The applications of gametogenesis challenge us to grapple with complex ethical questions, demanding a thoughtful and informed response that integrates scientific understanding with moral and theological principles. As society navigates these uncharted waters, the Church's role in guiding the ethical exploration of gametogenesis remains indispensable, offering a vision of hope and moral integrity in the face of the profound challenges and opportunities presented by this burgeoning field of biotechnology.

Ethical Challenges and Theological Responses

In navigating the intricate web of ethics surrounding gametogenesis, it becomes crucial to articulate the nuanced positions that the Church adheres to. This task is complex, not merely because of the scientific intricacies but also due to the ethical quandaries these technologies provoke. Gametogenesis, the artificial creation of gametes, presents a particularly acute ethical challenge within the sphere of reproductive technologies. As we delve into these issues, it's essential to consider both the scientific realities and the moral principles that guide our understanding and response.

The Church's teachings, deeply rooted in the dignity of human life and the sanctity of procreation, confront gametogenesis with significant skepticism. The creation of gametes outside of the natural biological context raises profound questions about the nature of parenthood, the rights of the child, and the very essence of human reproduction. These concerns aren't just abstract moral quandaries; they reflect deeply on the understanding of human life as a gift and the natural processes that bring it forth.

One of the primary ethical challenges revolves around the commodification of human life. Gametogenesis, by artificially creating gametes, could easily lead to scenarios where human eggs and sperm are produced, traded, and used in a manner that disassociates them from the human individuals they are meant to create. This commodification directly contradicts the Church's teachings on the inviolable dignity of every human being, from conception to natural death.

Another significant challenge lies in the potential for eugenic practices. The ability to create gametes in a lab opens the door to selecting and manipulating genetic traits, echoing the morally reprehensible eugenics movements of the past. Such practices, even when cloaked in the desire to eliminate genetic diseases, can perpetuate ideologies that view certain lives as more valuable than others based on genetic makeup.

The theological response to these challenges is multifaceted. It begins with a reaffirmation of the principle that life is a sacred gift from God, not a product to be manufactured. This principle is foundational, guiding the Church's approach to all bioethical issues, including gametogenesis. It emphasizes that every human being has inherent dignity and worth, irrespective of how they are conceived.

From this foundational principle flows the Church's concern for the sanctity of marriage and the procreative act. Procreation is understood not merely as a biological process but as a deeply personal act of love between a husband and wife. Gametogenesis, by creating human life outside the context of marital love, disrupts this understanding, treating life as a product of technology rather than a gift born of love.

The Church also voices concerns over the potential for exploitation and inequality gametogenesis could entail. The technology's expense and complexity could lead to a situation where only the wealthy have access to these means of reproduction, intensifying existing social inequalities and creating new forms of discrimination.

Furthermore, the unknown psychological and social impacts on children conceived through gametogenesis must be considered. These children might face complex questions about their identity, the nature of their conception, and their relationships with their parents and society. The Church's focus on the welfare of the child highlights the need for careful consideration of these long-term implications.

In response to these ethical challenges, the Church advocates for a framework that places the sanctity of human life and the dignity of procreation at the center. This involves rigorous moral discernment and a cautious approach to the adoption of new technologies. While the Church acknowledges the potential benefits of scientific advancements, it insists that these must not come at the cost of ethical principles and the welfare of the human person.

Dialogue between the Church, scientists, and ethicists is encouraged, aiming to foster a deeper understanding of the ethical dimensions of gametogenesis. The Church's teachings provide a moral compass, guiding these discussions towards considerations of equity, justice, and the common good.

Finally, the Church calls for comprehensive regulation and oversight of reproductive technologies, including gametogenesis. Such regulations should ensure that these technologies are used ethically, with respect for human dignity and the sanctity of life. Moreover, they should seek to prevent the commercialization of human life and the slippery slope toward eugenics.

In conclusion, the Church faces the challenges of gametogenesis with a nuanced ethical stance that emphasizes the dignity of human life, the sanctity of procreation, and the moral responsibility to use science for the true good of humanity. This approach does not categorically reject scientific advancement but rather seeks to integrate it within a moral framework that respects and upholds the fundamental values of human life and dignity.

In Vitro Fertilization: A Moral Examination

In the quest to understand the complex intersection between biotechnology and morality, in vitro fertilization (IVF) stands out as a poignant case study. This medical procedure, which involves combining an egg and sperm outside the body to create an embryo that is then implanted into the womb, has brought hope to countless couples struggling with infertility. Yet, from a Catholic ethical perspective, it raises profound questions about the sanctity of life, the natural law, and the moral limits of human intervention in the process of conception.

At the heart of the ethical debate on IVF is the Catholic Church's unwavering principle that life begins at conception. This belief underscores the intrinsic value of every human being from the first moment of existence. The process of IVF, however, routinely involves the creation of multiple embryos, not all of which are transferred to the womb. The fate of the remaining embryos—often frozen, discarded, or used for research— brings to light serious moral concerns about respect for human life and the commodification of human beings (Pope Paul VI Institute, 2023). These actions are seen as fundamentally inconsistent with the dignity accorded to human life in its embryonic stage, as articulated in Catholic teachings.

Further compounding these moral challenges is the aspect of natural law, a cornerstone of Catholic ethical reasoning. Natural law holds that moral principles are derived from the natural order designed by the Creator. It emphasizes the importance of adhering to the natural purposes of human faculties and processes. IVF, by bypassing the conjugal act, is viewed as contravening the natural law, which ordains sexual union not only as a means of procreation but as an expression of the marital bond (ant, 2022). This departure from natural law raises questions about the moral implications of manipulating human reproduction, even with noble intentions such as overcoming infertility.

The consideration of these ethical concerns should not overshadow the compassion and understanding due to couples experiencing the cross of infertility. The pain and longing for a child felt by many cannot be understated, and the Catholic moral tradition calls for empathy, support, and pastoral care in addressing these challenges. The

Church promotes open dialogues and seeks to guide individuals through the complexities of moral decision-making in light of Catholic teachings, encouraging exploration of morally licit alternatives such as adoption or natural family planning techniques (ant, 2017).

In conclusion, the moral examination of IVF through the lens of Catholic ethics underscores the tensions between technological advancements in reproduction and fundamental moral principles. This analysis reflects a broader struggle to navigate the ethical frontiers of biotechnology while adhering to the moral compass provided by faith. As the scientific community continues to push the boundaries of what is possible, the Catholic Church remains steadfast in its commitment to uphold the sanctity of life, the importance of natural law, and the dignity of human procreation.

Introduction to IVF and Its Implications for Catholic Ethics

At the heart of contemporary bioethical debates, In Vitro Fertilization (IVF) presents a complex matrix of moral, theological, and scientific concerns that challenge even the most steadfast ethical frameworks. Developed in 1978, IVF has since become a beacon of hope for couples struggling with infertility, yet it simultaneously raises profound ethical questions, particularly when examined through the lens of Catholic ethics. The practice involves the fertilization of an egg outside of the human body, a process that, while medically innovative, diverges from the natural procreative act valorized within Catholic teaching.

The Catholic Church, historically emphasizing the sanctity of life from conception, finds itself at an intricate crossroads when addressing the morality of IVF. This technology, by design, dissociates the procreative process from the marital act, a separation that has led to contentious debates within Catholic ethical circles. The Church's doctrine, rooted in the natural law theory, posits that human procreation should occur within the confines of marriage, an axiom that IVF, by its very nature, challenges.

Moreover, the process of IVF frequently involves the creation of multiple embryos, not all of which are transferred to the uterus. This surplus of embryos often leads to ethical dilemmas involving their future, including freezing, destruction, or use in research, each option carrying its own moral weight and implications. For the Church, which holds that life begins at conception and that each embryo possesses inherent dignity, these practices evoke serious moral reservations.

However, the desire for a child, felt keenly by many couples facing infertility, cannot be overlooked or dismissed as merely a quest for progeny. It is, at its core, a deeply human longing for continuation, belonging, and love. The pastoral response to such couples within the Catholic tradition requires a delicate balance, offering both understanding and moral guidance. Indeed, the Church advocates for the treatment of infertility through morally licit means, emphasizing methods that respect the dignity of the person and the sanctity of marriage.

The advent of IVF and its implications for Catholic ethics necessitate a thorough examination and discourse that is at once compassionate, informed, and principled. This entails delving into the intricacies of the technology itself, understanding its processes, successes, and limitations, while critically evaluating them against the backdrop of Catholic moral teaching. In doing so, one must consider the scientific aspects of IVF, including its techniques, the ethical considerations these raise, and the potential long-term effects on society, the family, and the individuals involved.

Furthermore, the discussion surrounding IVF and Catholic ethics is not confined to theological discourse alone. It invites a broader conversation involving bioethics, law, medicine, and social justice. Each perspective offers unique insights that contribute to a more holistic understanding of the moral landscape shaped by IVF.

One must also consider the nuances of individual cases, recognizing the diversity of circumstances that lead couples to consider IVF. This requires a pastoral sensitivity to the pain of infertility, the hope that IVF presents, and the moral conflict it may provoke. The

Catholic ethical response, therefore, must extend beyond abstract principles, engaging with the lived realities of those it seeks to guide.

In addressing the ethical implications of IVF, the question of human dignity invariably emerges as central. Viewing the embryo as a human life from the moment of conception, the Church's ethical stance concerns the protection and respect of this nascent human dignity. This perspective fundamentally shapes the Catholic approach to issues such as embryo selection and genetic testing, which are often integral to IVF protocols.

Additionally, the ethical considerations of IVF from a Catholic viewpoint extend into the realm of social and distributive justice. Questions regarding the accessibility of IVF treatments, the allocation of medical resources, and the societal implications of assisted reproductive technologies invite a critical examination of how such practices align with the Church's commitment to the common good and the preferential option for the poor.

The conversation surrounding IVF and Catholic ethics is also influenced by developments in genetic engineering and biotechnology. The potential for pre-implantation genetic diagnosis (PGD) alongside IVF to select for or against certain genetic traits introduces further ethical complexities. These emerging capabilities intersect with long-standing moral concerns regarding the nature of human intervention in procreation and the potential for 'designer babies.'

Despite the myriad ethical challenges IVF presents, it remains imperative that the discourse maintains a tone of empathy and understanding. The moral examination of IVF within Catholic ethics does not solely aim to delineate permissible actions but also to foster a compassionate engagement with those grappling with infertility, seeking paths that honor both their longing for parenthood and their adherence to moral principles.

In the final analysis, the intersection of IVF and Catholic ethics invites a profound reflection on the nature of human procreation, the values we place on human life, and the ways in which technology can both challenge and conform to these values. Navigating this complex terrain requires an attentive and nuanced approach, informed by both scientific understanding and ethical discernment.

In conclusion, as the Catholic Church and its faithful grapple with the ethical implications of IVF, the pursuit of moral clarity and compassionate pastoral care remains paramount. The dialogue betwixt faith and reason, tradition and innovation, provides a fertile ground for developing ethical responses that respect the dignity of human life, the sanctity of marriage, and the heartfelt desires of those yearning for a child. Through such dialogue, the Catholic community seeks not only to address the moral issues at hand but also to illuminate a path forward that is both ethically sound and profoundly humane.

Life Begins at Conception: Analyzing the Moral Issues of IVF

In the discourse of bioethics within the Catholic tradition, the sanctity of human life from its very inception at conception forms a foundational pillar. This tenet shapes our understanding and critiques of reproductive technologies, most notably in vitro fertilization (IVF). IVF, while a beacon of hope for many facing infertility, introduces complex moral considerations that warrant careful examination.

The process of IVF involves the fertilization of an egg outside the woman's body and the subsequent implantation of the embryo into the uterus. This technical bypassing of natural conception raises immediate concerns regarding the manipulation of human life at its most vulnerable stages.

At the heart of this moral quandary is the conviction that life begins at conception. This belief is not solely a religious or philosophical position but is increasingly supported by biological evidence showing the continuity and uniqueness of human life from the moment of conception. The production of human embryos in a laboratory setting for the purpose of implantation, research, or even destruction contravenes the inviolable dignity accorded to human life.

Moreover, the practice of selecting embryos based on desired traits or the likelihood of a successful pregnancy introduces a utilitarian calculus into the creation of human life. This selection process, often involving the discarding of embryos deemed less viable, further entrenches a view of human life as a commodity to be optimized rather than a sacred gift to be received with openness and reverence.

Another critical concern is the fate of surplus embryos. These embryos, frozen and stored, exist in a state of indefinite limbo, neither developing nor being allowed to fulfill their inherent potential of life. This situation presents a moral dilemma about the respect and care owed to these nascent forms of human life.

The Catholic ethical framework, informed by principles of natural law and the doctrine of the sanctity of human life, offers a critical perspective on these issues. It challenges the notion that the ends of alleviating infertility justify the means employed, especially when these means involve the instrumentalization of human life.

Additionally, the emotional and physical toll of IVF procedures on women cannot be overlooked. The process often involves invasive procedures and a regimen of hormonal treatments that pose health risks and impose significant burdens. The moral discourse around IVF must consider the welfare and dignity of women as integral to its analysis.

The Catholic Church advocates for alternatives that align with the moral principles guarding human dignity and the sanctity of conception. Natural family planning techniques and adoption are promoted as means to address infertility that accord with the moral order and respect the procreative purpose of marital intimacy.

While empathizing with the profound desire for parenthood that drives many towards IVF, the Catholic ethical tradition calls for a broader societal commitment to addressing infertility. This includes research into its causes, prevention, and treatments that do not compromise ethical principles. The challenge is to uphold the sanctity of life while responding compassionately to the suffering that infertility can cause.

Regarding policy and legislation, there is a pressing need for frameworks that govern reproductive technologies in a manner that respects human dignity. This includes regulations on the creation, use, and disposition of human embryos, ensuring that life at all stages is protected and valued.

The moral issues surrounding IVF also prompt deeper reflection on the meaning of parenthood and the openness to life. The Catholic perspective emphasizes that parenthood is a vocation, a calling that may be fulfilled in various ways, including through the care for and adoption of children who lack a family.

In conclusion, the moral examination of IVF from the perspective that life begins at conception unveils significant ethical concerns. These concerns are not merely abstract theological positions but have profound implications for how society values and respects human life at its most incipient stage.

The Church's role in this ongoing dialogue is not to condemn, but to offer a vision of human dignity and procreation that upholds the sanctity of life. In doing so, it invites a reevaluation of the methods society employs to address infertility, advocating for approaches that fully respect the dignity of human life and the ethical principles that shepherd its protection.

Through a marriage of scientific insights and moral reflection, this discourse challenges the current paradigms of reproductive technology. It beckons us towards a future where every human life, from conception to natural death, is cherished and protected.

The Moral Evils of Eugenics and Designer Babies

The quest for genetic perfection, a notion steeped in both historical and contemporary efforts, finds its most controversial application in the realms of eugenics and the creation of designer babies. These practices, ostensibly aimed at improving the human gene pool or granting individuals the ability to predetermine the genetic attributes of their offspring, carry with them profound moral implications. It's imperative to unravel the ethical fallacies that underpin these pursuits to truly comprehend the gravity of their moral failings. The principle of the inherent dignity of every human being, a cornerstone of Catholic ethical teachings, starkly contrasts with the reductionist view of human life as merely a collection of genetic traits that can be selected or discarded based on societal or personal preferences.

Central to the ethical critique of eugenics and the concept of designer babies is the understanding that these practices implicitly endorse a flawed notion of human perfection and worth. By placing undue emphasis on certain genetic characteristics, whether they be physical, intellectual, or otherwise, these practices perpetuate dangerous ideologies of superiority and inferiority. This not only contravenes the Catholic doctrine that sees divine image in every individual, regardless of their genetic makeup, but it also revives historical prejudices under a modern guise. Indeed, the pursuit of a 'perfect' genetic lineage harks back to the darkest chapters of eugenics in the 20th century, where similar ideologies led to egregious violations of human rights (ant, 2022).

From a philosophical standpoint, the manipulation of genetic material to produce designer babies or to engage in acts of eugenics raises significant concerns about human agency and authenticity. If one's genetic traits are chosen from a catalogue by another, can true autonomy and self-determination be said to exist? This dilemma probes the very essence of human freedom and individuality, suggesting that the resulting being is more a product of engineering than a unique person with an unrepeatable essence. Furthermore, such practices commodify life, reducing the sacred act of creation to a transactional exchange, thereby eroding the sanctity and mystery that surround the conception of new life (Davis, 2019).

The Catholic Church's response to these moral quandaries, as guided by its bioethical principles, emphasizes the inviolability of human life and the importance of safeguarding its innate dignity from conception to natural death. The Church denounces eugenics and the manufacture of designer babies as moral evils, not only because they disrupt the natural order, but also because they embody a profound disrespect for life. The Church urges society to consider the long-term ramifications of these practices, including the potential for new forms of discrimination and the widening of socioeconomic divides as genetic enhancements become yet another resource for the wealthy to exploit (Vatican Dicastery for Life, 2020).

In navigating the ethical landscape of genetic engineering, it is essential to maintain a balance between the promise of medical advancements and the preservation of moral values. The allure of genetically 'improved' offspring must not blind society to the inherent worth and dignity of every human life, in all its diversity and imperfection. As we advance into new genetic frontiers, let us be guided by a moral compass that prioritizes compassion, respect, and equity, drawing from both scientific understanding and the rich depths of ethical inquiry.

The Quest for Perfection: Ethical Fallacies

In the endeavor to achieve physical and intellectual superiority, humanity stands at the precipice of a slippery slope. The modern zeitgeist, propelled by advances in genetic technologies, particularly CRISPR-Cas9, has reignited a quasi-Promethean ambition to surpass our natural genetic endowment in pursuit of a utopian ideal of perfection. This ambition, while appealing at first glance, opens a Pandora's box of ethical dilemmas and moral ambiguities, particularly in the context of eugenics and the creation of 'designer babies'.

The allure of eugenic practices is not a novelty in human history. From the Spartan abandonment of 'imperfect' infants to the sinister endeavors of the 20th-century eugenics movements, the quest for a 'better' human species has perilously intertwined with the darkest episodes of human history. Today, the tools might have evolved, but the underpinning ethos—seeking to control, predict, and perfect human life—remains eerily similar, hence morally questionable. The desire to eliminate suffering and enhance human abilities presents a facade of benevolence yet fails to comprehend the intrinsic value of diversity and the unpredictability of life, which are central to the human experience.

Genetic interventions in the form of 'designer babies' signify a fundamental departure from the acceptance of life as a gift into a commodified, engineered artifact. This shift is not merely semantic but reflects a profound ontological transformation in how life is conceived and valued. By valuating certain genetic traits over others, we inadvertently step onto a slippery slope towards a new form of eugenics, thinly veiled under the promise of health and prosperity.

It is imperative to question: what criteria govern this quest for perfection? Physical prowess, intellectual acumen, or resistance to disease? And who decides? The specter of societal inequalities looms large over these questions, heralding a future where genetic enhancements exacerbate existing disparities rather than ameliorating them. The meritocratic guise of genetic enhancement belies a stark reality; it privileges those who can afford it, leaving behind a stratum of society perpetually disadvantaged, not by nature, but by human design.

From a deontological standpoint, the intentional selection and alteration of genes for non-therapeutic purposes infringe upon the Kantian principle of treating humanity both in one's own person and in the person of another always as an end and never merely as a means. This reduction of human life to a set of desirable traits, which can be cherry-picked and implanted, erodes the inherent dignity and respect owed to every person.

This quest for perfection, under the guise of freedom of choice, paradoxically imprisons humanity within an indefinable and unattainable ideal. What constitutes perfection is perennially elusive, shaped by cultural, temporal, and societal shifts. The risk is substantial; in striving for an ideal, we may lose sight of the inherent worth and dignity of the individual, regardless of their genetic constitution.

Moreover, the relentless pursuit of genetic enhancement underestimates the role of environmental, social, and educational factors in shaping individuals. By placing undue emphasis on genetic determinism, we risk neglecting the societal structures that profoundly influence human development and perpetuating a myth of genetic inevitability that undermines the human capacity for growth, change, and resilience.

The theological critique further enriches this conversation, positing that the quest for perfection through human manipulation usurps the creative prerogative of the Divine. In the Catholic tradition, every human life, with its imperfections and limitations, is imbued with inherent dignity and value. To attempt to 'improve' upon God's creation through genetic manipulation is to tread into a domain reserved for the Creator, neglecting the sanctity and mystery of life.

Additionally, the ethical fallacy of presuming to predict and control the outcome of genetic manipulation overlooks the complexity of the human genome. The intricacies of gene interactions and expressions are not fully understood, and interventions carry the risk of unforeseen consequences, not only for the individual but for subsequent generations.

The narrative of genetic perfectionism also plays into a dangerous fallacy: the belief in ultimate control over nature. This hubris ignores the lessons of history and the inherent unpredictability of complex biological systems. The quest for control could ultimately render humanity more vulnerable, not less, to genetic and environmental uncertainties.

In conclusion, the quest for perfection through genetic manipulation, while seductive in its promise, is fraught with ethical fallacies and moral ambiguities. It behooves us, as a society, to proceed with caution, grounded in a deep respect for the inherent dignity of all human life. By fostering a culture that values diversity and inclusivity, we can navigate the genetic frontier without succumbing to the siren calls of eugenics and designer babies.

Perfection, in the end, may lie not in the eradication of all imperfections but in the embrace of the diversity that constitutes the human condition. It is here, in the mosaic of human life, that true progress and enlightenment lie, not in the pursuit of an illusory and unattainable ideal.

Catholic Responses to the New Eugenics

As we delve into the Catholic Church's positioning on contemporary eugenic practices, which include gene editing and the creation of designer babies, it's fundamental to revisit the ethical frameworks that have historically informed the Church's teachings. At the heart of these teachings is the inviolable sanctity of human life, a theme that consistently guides the Church's responses to the moral quandaries posed by modern genetic technologies.

The notion of creating a so-called "perfect" human through genetic manipulation raises immediate red flags within Catholic bioethics. The Church views each life as inherently valuable, bestowed with dignity from the moment of conception (Pontifical Academy for Life, 2023). The pursuit of perfection through genetic selection or alteration treads perilously close to a rejection of this divine gift, suggesting that some lives are more valuable than others based on arbitrary genetic characteristics.

This modern incarnation of eugenics, albeit cloaked in the promising veneer of eliminating hereditary diseases, does not escape the moral pitfalls of its predecessors. The Church's response is not merely reactionary but deeply philosophical, recognizing the essential equality and brotherhood of all humans. This perspective finds its roots in natural law, a principle which undergirds much of Catholic ethical thinking, proposing that certain rights and moral values are inherent in human nature and can be discerned through reason (Doudna & Charpentier, 2016).

The slippery slope of enhancing human traits through genetic modification also prompts the Church to question where the line is drawn. If we begin by correcting what are deemed as "undesirable" genetic traits, at what point does the pursuit of enhancement undermine our acceptance and love of the "imperfect" human being? This mirrors a societal impulsion towards a homogenized ideal of perfection, veering dangerously close to playing God—a role that Catholicism reserves solely for the Creator.

Moreover, the concept of designer babies raises significant questions about parental responsibility and the nature of unconditional love. The Church's teaching stresses that love, especially parental love, is by its nature unconditional, welcoming the child as a unique, unrepeatable gift (Pontifical Academy for Life, 2023). The move towards selecting or altering a child's genetic makeup introduces conditions to this love, suggesting it can be calibrated based on predetermined traits or capabilities.

Scientific advances such as CRISPR-Cas9, while holding remarkable potential for gene therapy, further compound the ethical complexities. The Church acknowledges the profound benefits these technologies may offer in curing genetic diseases. However, it insists that such interventions must always respect the dignity of the person and the sanctity of life. The distinction between therapeutic and non-therapeutic interventions becomes crucial here, with the Church advocating for the former while expressing grave concerns over the latter, primarily when used for enhancement purposes (ant, 2017).

The Catholic response to these new eugenic practices also emphasizes the importance of equitable access to genetic therapies. The principle of the common good, a key component of Catholic social teaching, impels us to consider who benefits from these technologies and at what cost. The Church cautions against a future where genetic enhancements are available only to those with means, thereby exacerbating social inequalities and creating a genetic underclass (Pontifical Academy for Life, 2023).

In addressing gametogenesis and in vitro fertilization (IVF), the Church's teachings are consistent with its broader ethical stance on the sanctity of life and the natural law. IVF, particularly, is problematic from a Catholic perspective due to the separation of procreation from the marital act, and the potential for the commodification of human life. With gametogenesis offering the possibility of creating human eggs and sperm from other cell types, the Church is concerned about the further detachment of procreation from its natural, divinely intended context (Doudna & Charpentier, 2016).

The Church's teachings are not intended to stifle scientific progress or deny the suffering of those with inheritable diseases. Rather, they provide a moral compass, guiding humanity as we navigate the complex ethical terrain of genetic modification. The fundamental question posed is whether these technologies serve the true dignity and vocation of the human person, as understood through a Christian anthropological lens.

As we continue to confront the ethical challenges presented by advancements in genetics, the Church calls for a dialogue between science and faith. Such a dialogue is essential not only for addressing the moral dilemmas at hand but also for ensuring that scientific progress reflects a holistic understanding of the human person. Engaging in this conversation, the Church advocates for a science that is truly at the service of humanity, promoting the integral development of every person and the entire person.

In conclusion, the Catholic Church's response to the new eugenics is measured and principled, rooted in a profound respect for the sanctity of life and the innate dignity of each individual. As we forge ahead into new genetic frontiers, these teachings invite us to reflect on the kind of world we wish to create for future generations. Will it be a world that values individuals solely based on their genetic makeup, or one that recognizes the intrinsic worth of every person, regardless of their physical or genetic characteristics? The answer to this question will significantly shape the fabric of our society in the years to come.

Chapter 7: The Sanctity of Life in the Age of Genetic Manipulation

In an era where the boundaries of life can be rewritten at the molecular level, the sanctity of life emerges as a principle under siege. As developments in genetic manipulation technologies, such as CRISPR-Cas9, unfold at a breathtaking pace, ethical reflections grounded in the dignity of human life are imperative. The Catholic tradition, with its deep reverence for the sanctity of life from conception to natural death, offers a rich ethical framework for navigating these groundbreaking advancements. This chapter delves into the critical examination of how contemporary genetic manipulation practices, while promising in their potential to eradicate diseases, simultaneously pose significant moral dilemmas that challenge our fundamental understanding of life itself.

The practice of genetic editing, particularly in human embryos, brings to the forefront questions about the intrinsic value of human life and the limits of human intervention. While the potential to prevent genetic diseases can be seen as a laudable goal, the moral quandaries surrounding the alteration of germline cells create a complex ethical landscape. The issue is not just about the immediate effects of these manipulations but also about the long-term implications for humanity. Moreover, the prospect of creating so-called "designer babies" raises profound concerns regarding the commodification of human life and the potential for new forms of inequality and discrimination. These ethical considerations force us to grapple with the essence of what it means to be human and the respect due to every individual as a unique creation, irrespective of genetic composition (Sandel, 2007).

Amidst these challenges, the Catholic ethical tradition serves as a guiding light, emphasizing the principle of respect for life and cautioning against overreaching human autonomy that disregards the natural moral order. Through careful analysis of specific case studies, including gene therapies and genetic enhancements, this chapter seeks to illuminate the moral boundaries that should govern our engagement with genetic technologies. By fostering a dialogue that respects both scientific innovation and the sanctity of life, we can navigate the complex ethical terrain of genetic manipulation in a manner that upholds human dignity and the common good.

Preserving Human Dignity Amidst Biotechnological Advances

In an era where biotechnological advancements proceed at an unprecedented pace, it becomes ever more critical to ensure that the sanctity of human life remains at the forefront of the discussion. The rapid development in genetic manipulation technologies brings with it a plethora of ethical considerations, paramount among these being the preservation of human dignity. It is within this context that we find ourselves grappling with the moral implications of our ability to edit the very blueprint of life.

The development of CRISPR-Cas9 technology has, undeniably, opened new frontiers in genetic research, allowing scientists to edit parts of the genome by removing, adding, or altering sections of the DNA sequence. While the potential for curing genetic diseases, improving crops, and even eradicating pests is immense, the ethical ramifications cannot be overlooked. The capacity to alter life at its most fundamental level introduces a range of ethical dilemmas centered around the intrinsic dignity of the human person.

The Catholic ethical framework, with its emphasis on the sanctity of life and the inherent dignity of every human being, provides a critical lens through which to examine these biotechnological advances. This framework does not merely reject all forms of genetic manipulation outright but rather seeks to discern their use in a manner that respects human dignity, promotes the common good, and adheres to natural law principles.

One of the primary concerns with genetic editing technologies, such as CRISPR, is the slippery slope towards eugenics and designer babies. The quest for perfection, through the elimination of undesirable traits or the enhancement of desirable ones, raises significant ethical questions. The critical issue here is not just the potential to alter human nature but also the implications for social justice and equality. The ability to edit human embryos could lead to a society where only the wealthy have access to technologies that prevent genetic diseases or enhance certain traits, thereby widening the gap between the rich and the poor and infringing upon the equal dignity of all persons.

In this light, the Catholic Church's teachings offer a profound insight into the responsible stewardship of genetic technologies. The Church neither condemns nor blindly accepts such technologies but rather advocates for their use in a manner that is respectful of life's sacredness from conception to natural death. This perspective emphasizes healing and improving human life without manipulating it at its very core in ways that compromise inherent human dignity.

Gametogenesis and in vitro fertilization (IVF) present additional ethical challenges within the context of Catholic bioethics. These reproductive technologies, while offering hope to many who struggle with infertility, also pose questions about the sanctity of life and the natural law. The Church's stance on these issues is guided by a principle that respects the procreative and unitive purposes of marriage, raising concerns about the moral implications of creating life outside the traditional marital act.

The possibility of IVF leading to the commodification of human life, where embryos are created, selected, and often discarded, further illustrates the moral pitfalls associated with these technologies. The Catholic ethical perspective therefore mandates that these technologies must always uphold the dignity of the human person, from conception onwards, and avoid reducing human life to a mere means to an end.

The concepts of gene editing and designer babies venture into the realm of eugenics, a notion unequivocally condemned in Catholic teaching. The Church's strong stance against eugenics stems from its advocacy for the equal dignity of all human lives, irrespective of their genetic makeup. This perspective is integral to ensuring that biotechnological advances serve to heal and enhance human life without discriminating against individuals based on their genetic traits.

Moreover, the application of genetic modification in agriculture and environmental conservation presents another dimension to the ethical debate. While the potential benefits for food security and ecosystem management are significant, caution is necessary to ensure these technologies do not inadvertently harm the environment or lead to unforeseen consequences. The Catholic view, which holds a deep reverence for creation, insists that such interventions must always consider the long-term impacts on the planet and its inhabitants.

In conclusion, the path forward requires a delicate balance between harnessing the potential of biotechnological advances and preserving the sanctity of human life and the natural order. The Catholic ethical framework, with its emphasis on human dignity, the common good, and respect for creation, provides an invaluable guide for navigating these complex moral landscapes. As we venture further into the age of genetic manipulation, it is imperative that these ethical considerations remain at the forefront of our decision-making processes, ensuring that technological progress does not come at the expense of our most fundamental ethical principles.

Ultimately, the journey through the terrain of genetic manipulation demands vigilant discernment, underpinned by a commitment to upholding the intrinsic value of life at every turn. The promise of biotechnological advances brings with it a responsibility to wield these powerful tools wisely, in ways that honor the dignity of the human person and contribute to the flourishing of all creation. In this quest, the teachings of the Catholic Church offer not only caution but also hope, reminding us that amidst the complex ethical dilemmas of our time, the sanctity of life remains an inviolable principle that guides us toward a more just, compassionate, and dignified world.

Case Studies: Moral Dilemmas in Genetic Editing

In the pursuit of understanding the moral landscape sculpted by the advances in genetic manipulation, it becomes imperative to delve into specific instances where these ethical conflicts manifest vividly. This examination of case studies illuminates the treacherous terrain between scientific innovation and moral considerations. Each situation underscores a unique dilemma rooted in the sanctity of life, echoing the complexities faced in the age of genetic manipulation.

The first of these dilemmas involves an instance where a couple, after undergoing genetic screening, discovers their unborn child carries the gene for Huntington's Disease—a fatal condition that manifests in adulthood. The possibility of utilizing CRISPR technology to correct the gene and spare the child a predestined fate of suffering seems, at first glance, a mercy. However, the procedure's ethical implications, from the perspective of altering human essence to the unforeseeable risks, unveil layers of moral questioning.

Another case challenges the ethical bounds with the use of gene editing to enhance human attributes—such as intelligence, physical strength, or aesthetic qualities— rather than curing disease. This leap from therapeutic to enhancement purposes raises a myriad of concerns regarding natural law, human dignity, and the intrinsic value of individuals regardless of their capabilities or appearances.

A particularly poignant scenario arises with the advent of designer babies, where prospective parents might opt to choose non-medical traits for their children. Beyond the immediate ethical discomfort this notion brings, it provokes a deeper examination of parental love's unconditional nature and the societal implications of such choices, potentially paving the way for new forms of discrimination.

In reflecting on therapeutic uses, one case spotlights a revolutionary gene therapy for a rare, debilitating disease fraught with immense suffering. The moral evaluation here weighs the significant benefits against potential unforeseeable consequences, the sanctity of intervening in the human genome, and considerations regarding the equitable distribution of such treatments.

The contemplation extends to instances of somatic versus germline editing, where modifications made in somatic cells affect only the individual, whereas germline alterations are inheritable. This distinction brings forth multifaceted ethical considerations regarding consent, ramifications for future generations, and the intrinsic moral responsibilities toward those not yet born.

Amid these considerations, one encounters the dilemma of using genetic editing technologies in embryonic research. The imperative to advance scientific knowledge competes with the ethical obligation to respect embryonic life, raising profound questions about when human life gains moral value and the consequential status of embryos in research contexts.

The use of gene drives in disease vector organisms, aimed at eliminating threats like malaria, presents another case where the potential for immense benefit to humanity is tinged with ethical uncertainty. The radical alteration of ecosystems and the unpredictability of long-term effects introduce a moral obligation to balance human welfare with respect for nature's integrity.

A case of gene editing to prevent mitochondrial disease by creating embryos with three genetic parents—introducing mitochondrial DNA from a donor into the egg—underscores questions of identity, the definition of parenthood, and unforeseen consequences on genetic inheritance.

Each of these case studies not only showcases the spectrum of genetic editing's potential but also brings to the forefront the deep moral inquiries invoked by such capabilities. Through the prism of these dilemmas, one confronts the central issue of human dignity and the sanctity of life amidst the allure of biotechnological progress.

The moral fabric of society is inevitably tested by the evolution of genetic technologies. These case studies serve as a reminder of the complexity and gravity of ethical decision-making in the context of genetic manipulation. They demand a discourse that is profoundly informed, critically engaged, and deeply reflective of our values as a civilization, particularly within the context of Catholic moral teaching.

Understanding these dilemmas through the lens of Catholic bioethics necessitates a commitment to the principles of human dignity, the sanctity of life, and the common good. It requires a discerning evaluation of the moral and ethical dimensions of genetic editing, grounded in a theology that respects the gift of creation while navigating the challenges posed by scientific advancements.

The exploration of these case studies not only enriches the ethical discourse around genetic editing but also empowers individuals and communities to engage with these moral complexities from a place of informed conscience and ethical integrity. It is through such rigorous examination that society can hope to tread the precarious path between harnessing the potential of genetic technologies and upholding the sanctity of human life.

Chapter 8: Healthcare, Genetics, and the Poor

In the progressing narrative of modern genetics and healthcare, a salient yet often sidestepped concern is the stark inequity in access to emerging genetic therapies and treatments. This chapter delves into the ramifications of such disparities, especially their impact on the underprivileged sectors of society. This discourse is steeped in the Catholic ethical tradition, which underscores a preferential option for the poor and vulnerable. The complex interplay between revolutionary genetic technologies and social justice presents a moral landscape fraught with challenges and opportunities for advocacy.

The promise of genetic technologies, such as CRISPR-Cas9, to cure debilitating genetic disorders is tempered by the reality of their accessibility. The burgeoning field of gene therapy, despite its potential, has illuminated a stark divide. This divide is not merely scientific but profoundly social and ethical. The cost of these therapies, often exorbitant, effectively places them out of reach for a significant portion of the global population (Doudna & Charpentier, 2016). The preferential option for the poor, a principle deeply woven into Catholic social teaching, challenges the current healthcare paradigm by advocating for a system where the needs of the poor take precedence over the desires of the wealthy.

Genetic medicine's advancements illuminate a path toward previously unimaginable possibilities for treating genetic diseases. Yet, this path seems littered with obstacles for the poor, casting a long shadow on the ideals of equity and justice. The discourse surrounding genetics and healthcare must, therefore, grapple with the question of how to bridge this chasm of disparity. It's imperative to explore mechanisms for redistributing our scientific achievements more equitably, ensuring that the miraculous benefits of genetic medicine are accessible to all, regardless of socioeconomic status (Evans, 2019).

This chapter thus embarks on a philosophical exploration into the nature of healthcare as a fundamental human right, arguing that access to genetic treatments should not be predicated on wealth or social standing. This argument is framed within the Catholic understanding of the common good and the inherent dignity of every human life. The moral weight of this argument is rooted in the assertion that scientific advancements in healthcare carry the obligation of universal benefit, especially for the least among us.

In light of the preferential option for the poor, this discourse challenges the market-driven paradigm that currently dominates the genetic medicine industry. The ethical quandary here involves a critique of the structures that perpetuate inequality, suggesting that a more communal approach to healthcare resources could pave the way for more equitable access. Such a proposition invokes a critical reevaluation of our societal priorities and the values that underpin our economic systems.

Through a blend of descriptive narrative, scientific analysis, and philosophical inquiry, this chapter seeks to unravel the complexities at the intersection of genetics, healthcare, and social justice. The conversation necessarily ventures into discussions about policy-making, advocating for reforms that are informed by a robust ethical framework. This involves not only making genetic treatments more affordable but also investing in public health infrastructure that can support widespread access to these life-saving technologies.

Moreover, the discourse confronts the ethical implications of prioritizing certain diseases over others based on profitability and market demand. This presents a moral conundrum that challenges the very foundations of our healthcare systems, pushing the reader to consider the value of human life in terms beyond monetary and market-driven metrics. It is a call to envision a healthcare landscape where every life is given equal consideration, and where the advancements in genetic medicine serve the global community indiscriminately.

The Catholic ethical perspective, with its emphasis on human dignity and social justice, provides a unique lens through which to examine the dilemmas presented by modern genetic technologies. This chapter, therefore, not only critiques the current state of affairs but also offers a vision for a more just and equitable future. It is an invitation to engage in a dialogue that transcends disciplinary boundaries, encouraging collaboration between ethicists, scientists, policymakers, and advocates for the poor.

In conclusion, "Healthcare, Genetics, and the Poor" navigates through the intricate moral landscape shaped by the intersection of genetics and social justice. It calls for a concerted effort to ensure that the fruits of genetic medicine do not exacerbate existing inequalities but rather become a catalyst for bridging gaps and fostering a more inclusive society. The chapter embodies a hope that the advancements in genetic technologies can be harnessed for the common good, echoing the Catholic call to care for the most vulnerable among us.

Unequal Access: Social Justice Issues in Genetic Therapies

In the realm of healthcare and genetic therapies, the divide between the haves and the have-nots has only deepened with advancements in technology. As we delve into the complexities surrounding the accessibility of genetic therapies, it's paramount to address the ethical and social justice issues that emerge. The discussion here is framed around the fundamental belief in the inherent dignity of every human being and the moral imperative to ensure equitable access to healthcare advancements.

Genetic therapies, heralded as groundbreaking treatments for a range of debilitating diseases, present a double-edged sword. On one hand, they offer hope for curing previously intractable conditions. On the other, their exorbitant costs and the complexities involved in their development and distribution have led to a situation where only a fraction of the global population can benefit from them. This disparity raises critical questions about the principles of justice, equity, and the common good in the context of modern healthcare.

One of the core issues at the heart of this debate is the stark inequality in accessing these therapies. In affluent nations, patients might encounter fewer barriers to access, albeit still facing significant hurdles including insurance coverage limitations and high out-of-pocket expenses. Meanwhile, in low to middle-income countries, such therapies are often nothing more than a distant dream, inaccessible due to their prohibitive costs and the lack of healthcare infrastructure to support their delivery.

The preferential option for the poor, a principle deeply ingrained in the ethos of caring and justice, demands a reevaluation of how genetic therapies are developed, priced, and distributed. The moral imperative suggests that societies and the entities within them, including governments, healthcare institutions, and the biotech industry, bear a collective responsibility to ensure that innovations in healthcare serve the common good, especially the needs of the most vulnerable among us.

Moreover, the current model of funding and incentives in the biopharmaceutical industry often prioritizes diseases that are prevalent in wealthier countries, overlooking conditions that primarily affect poor populations. This skewed focus not only exacerbates existing health inequities but also neglects the moral call to address the suffering of the "least of these."

There's also a critical need to explore and implement innovative financing and partnership models that can reduce the cost barriers associated with genetic therapies. Strategies such as tiered pricing, where the cost of drugs is adjusted based on a country's ability to pay, and patent pools, which can enable generic manufacturing of expensive drugs, are options that warrant serious consideration.

Public policy plays a pivotal role in shaping the landscape of genetic therapy access. Policies that support research into diseases affecting marginalized populations, along with regulations that encourage the development of affordable therapies, are crucial steps towards bridging the access gap.

Within the context of Catholic social teaching, the conversation around genetic therapies and access echoes the broader theme of healthcare as a basic human right. The preferential option for the poor not only highlights the moral responsibility to prioritize the needs of the marginalized but also challenges the commodification of healthcare, asserting that profit should never come at the expense of human dignity and the sanctity of life.

Engagement with community stakeholders, including patients, healthcare providers, and ethicists, is essential in crafting policies and practices that reflect the values of equity and justice. Listening to the voices of those directly impacted by the access divide can provide valuable insights into the barriers they face and the solutions that would best meet their needs.

Moreover, the ethical imperative to ensure equitable access to genetic therapies extends beyond national borders. International cooperation and solidarity are critical in addressing the global disparities in health outcomes. Initiatives that foster collaboration between countries, such as global health partnerships and international funding mechanisms, can play a significant role in making genetic therapies more accessible worldwide.

The pursuit of equitable access to genetic therapies also calls for a critical examination of intellectual property rights. While these rights are designed to protect and incentivize innovation, they can also hinder the availability of life-saving treatments. Balancing the rights of innovators with the needs of the global community is a complex ethical challenge that requires careful consideration and nuanced solutions.

In conclusion, the conversation around unequal access to genetic therapies is not just a matter of scientific or economic deliberation but fundamentally a moral and ethical one. It's a reflection of how societies value human life and dignity, particularly of those most in need. As advancements in genetic therapies continue to evolve, so too must the commitment to ensuring that these innovations serve the common good, offering hope and healing to all, regardless of their economic standing.

The moral landscape of healthcare and genetic therapies is one marked by profound challenges but also by the enduring promise of compassion, justice, and solidarity. Moving forward, it's imperative that all stakeholders, guided by these principles, work tirelessly to bridge the gap in access, not merely as a matter of policy but as a testament to the shared commitment to uphold the dignity and worth of every human being.

The Preferential Option for the Poor in Genetic Medicine

As our journey through the moral implications of genetics and bioethics continues, an essential aspect that necessitates a profound examination is the preferential option for the poor within the realm of genetic medicine. This concept, deeply embedded in Catholic social teaching, calls for a prioritization of the needs of the poor and vulnerable in every aspect of life, including the rapidly evolving field of genetic medicine. This chapter seeks to explore how this principle can be actualized in a world where advancements in genetic technologies are both promising and unsettling.

In the context of healthcare, especially genetic medicine, the preferential option for the poor challenges us to question: Who has access to these cutting-edge treatments? Genetic therapies, such as CRISPR, offer groundbreaking opportunities to address genetic disorders that have plagued humanity for centuries. Yet, the staggering costs and complex technologies involved place these treatments beyond the reach of the impoverished and marginalized. This disparity not only widens the gap in health equity but also raises profound ethical concerns regarding justice, fairness, and the intrinsic dignity of every human person.

The complexity of genetic medicine and its implications for the poor can't be understated. On one hand, there exists a moral obligation to advance scientific research and healthcare to eradicate diseases that disproportionately impact the poor. On the other hand, there's a risk that these advances may further entrench social inequalities if they remain inaccessible to those who bear the heaviest burden of genetic ailments. Thus, a moral tension arises between the potential for great good and the possibility of exacerbating existing injustices.

Consider the case of gene therapies currently in development for treating sickle cell disease, an inherited condition that significantly affects populations in sub-Saharan Africa and among African descents worldwide. These therapies represent a beacon of hope for eradicating a disease with a high toll on quality of life and life expectancy. However, the projected costs and healthcare infrastructure required for such treatments make them practically unattainable for the majority of those suffering from sickle cell disease in poorer regions.

This scenario exemplifies the critical need for a framework that prioritizes the poor in the allocation and development of genetic treatments. A genuine commitment to the preferential option for the poor in genetic medicine demands not only making these treatments accessible to all who need them but also ensuring that research and development efforts are directed towards conditions that predominantly affect the poor.

Moreover, ethical considerations must extend beyond accessibility and affordability. The dialogues surrounding genetic medicine often revolve around the potential for creating 'designer babies,' thus exacerbating a culture that seeks to eliminate imperfection. This culture, if unchecked, threatens to undervalue the lives of those who do not meet these artificially constructed ideals of perfection. Here, the preferential option for the poor serves as a critical counterbalance, reminding us that every life holds intrinsic value, and that those who society often views as 'less perfect' must be defended and prioritized in medical advancements.

Fulfilling the preferential option for the poor in genetic medicine also involves advocacy and policy-making. Policies must be crafted to ensure that genetic therapies are included in healthcare plans and coverage, particularly in low-income settings. International cooperation and public-private partnerships can play a significant role in subsidizing costs, facilitating technology transfer, and building the necessary infrastructure in resource-limited settings to make these life-saving treatments available and affordable.

Education and empowerment of the poor regarding genetic diseases and potential treatments are equally crucial. Misinformation and lack of awareness can hinder the uptake of genetic therapies even when they become accessible. Community engagement initiatives, culturally sensitive educational programs, and the involvement of local leaders and healthcare workers in disseminating information can help bridge this gap.

Moreover, the Catholic Church and other religious organizations have a pivotal role to play in actualizing the preferential option for the poor in genetic medicine. Through their extensive networks and influence, they can advocate for equitable policies, support research aimed at diseases prevalent in poor communities, and provide moral guidance on the ethical dimensions of genetic interventions.

In conclusion, as we stand on the cusp of a new era in genetic medicine, the moral imperative to prioritize the needs of the poor and vulnerable must be at the forefront of our endeavors. The preferential option for the poor is not merely an ideal but a practical guide that shapes how we develop, distribute, and deploy genetic therapies. It challenges us to envision a future where advancements in genetic medicine bridge rather than widen the chasm of health inequalities, ensuring that the fruits of genetic research are truly a blessing for all humanity.

As we navigate these uncharted waters, embracing the preferential option for the poor offers us both a moral compass and a transformative vision. It calls us to act justly, love tenderly, and walk humbly with our God, ensuring that in our quest to heal and enhance the human condition, we don't leave the least of our brothers and sisters behind.

Chapter 9: The Environment and Genetic Engineering

In the realms of modernity, where science and technology have bounded leaps into the unknown, we encounter the intersection of genetic engineering and the environment. Our stewardship of the land and its creatures entails a profound moral responsibility, particularly as we wield the tools of genetic manipulation. This chapter delves into the Catholic perspectives on genetic intervention in nature, underlining the essential conversations surrounding ethical considerations in agricultural biotechnology. It's a journey through the moral implications and responsibilities we hold within the tapestry of creation.

At the heart of genetic engineering's promise are enhancements in agricultural production, addressing challenges such as climate change, pestilence, and food security. Yet, through the lens of Catholic ethics, this technological prowess invokes critical scrutiny. The intrinsic value of creation, as posited in foundational Catholic teaching, suggests that any manipulation of nature must be evaluated not solely on its utility or profit margins but on its respect for the natural order and the welfare of all creation. As we delve into the genetic modification of crops and livestock, questions emerge about long-term environmental impacts, biodiversity, and the potential unforeseen consequences of such interventions.

The endeavor to align with Catholic ethical principles leads us to consider not just the "how" of genetic engineering but the "why." It invites a reflection on the motivation behind altering the genetic makeup of our environment—is it to genuinely address global hunger and environmental sustainability, or do profit motives overshadow the moral imperatives? The principle of the common good, a cornerstone in Catholic social teaching, provides a crucial lens through which to examine the deployment of genetically modified organisms. This principle urges a holistic approach, considering the impact on small-scale farmers, indigenous populations, and ecological systems, thus advocating for justice and equity in the distribution of biotechnological innovations.

The dialogue between science and faith, particularly on the frontiers of genetic engineering, is enriched by the Catholic tradition of 'care for our common home,' as emphasized in recent papal encyclicals. This care extends beyond human concerns, embracing all of creation as a sacred trust. As such, the manipulation of genetic material in plants and animals is not merely a technical issue but a theological and moral one, challenging us to reflect deeply on our role as co-creators with God. The ethical considerations in agricultural biotechnology are not static but evolve as our understanding of genetics and its implications for the environment and society deepen.

Conclusively, as we tread into the future of genetic engineering, the realms of Catholic ethics provide us with a compass. Through a thoughtful evaluation of both the advancements and the ethical dilemmas posed by genetic interventions in nature, we are called to navigate this complex terrain with a commitment to the dignity of all creation, the common good, and the ethical stewardship of our planet. In this light, genetic engineering can be viewed not merely as a tool of dominion but as an opportunity for responsible stewardship, in alignment with the moral and theological values that guide us.

Modifying Creation: Catholic Perspectives on Genetic Intervention in Nature

The contemplation of nature's grandeur, its intricate complexities, and the delicate balance sustaining life has long inspired awe and reverence. Within the framework of Catholic teaching, nature is perceived as a testament to the Creator's wisdom and benevolence, tasked to humanity for stewardship and care. This responsibility, deeply embedded in the Christian tradition, becomes particularly poignant in the context of genetic engineering. As the capabilities to modify the genetic fabric of living organisms advance, the Catholic perspective, with its rich tapestry of ethical considerations, offers a nuanced approach to the interventions in nature's design.

At the heart of Catholic bioethics is the recognition of the inherent dignity of all creation. This principle, foundational to understanding the Church's stance on genetic intervention, underscores the notion that all of creation bears the divine imprint and, as such, merits respect and protection. This respect extends beyond human life to encompass the entirety of the natural world, which includes animals, plants, and ecosystems. The manipulation of genetic material in nature, therefore, prompts critical ethical questions about the preservation of this dignity.

The advancement of genetic technologies such as CRISPR-Cas9 has ushered in unprecedented possibilities for addressing challenges in agriculture, disease control, and environmental conservation. Examples include developing crop varieties with enhanced nutritional value, resistance to pests and diseases, and the ability to withstand the harsh conditions attributed to climate change. While the potential benefits are considerable, the Catholic perspective insists on a discerning approach that weighs these outcomes against potential risks to ecological balance, species integrity, and the broader implications of humans exerting control over the genetic makeup of nature.

An important consideration in the Catholic discourse on genetic engineering is the principle of the common good. This principle, integral to Catholic social teaching, advocates for actions that benefit society as a whole, fostering the well-being of current and future generations. Genetic interventions in nature, from this viewpoint, should be evaluated based on their capacity to contribute to the sustainability of the environment, food security, and equitable access to benefits. The challenge lies in ensuring that such technological advancements do not exacerbate existing inequalities or lead to the exploitation of natural resources to the detriment of the environment or marginalized communities.

The concept of stewardship is another critical dimension of the Catholic approach to genetic intervention. Humanity's role as stewards, according to this understanding, involves a caretaking responsibility that respects natural processes and aims to preserve biodiversity. It calls for a precautionary approach to genetic engineering, where the long-term impacts on ecosystems and interdependent species are carefully considered. The urge to 'play God' by altering nature's genetics is met with a call for humility and prudence, acknowledging human limitations in fully understanding the complexities of ecological interactions and the potential for unintended consequences.

The Church does not outrightly condemn the use of genetic engineering in nature but emphasizes the need for moral discernment in guiding these interventions. This discernment is informed by a holistic understanding of creation's purpose, where technological advancements serve the common good, protect vulnerable species, and maintain ecological harmony. In navigating the moral landscape of genetic intervention, the Church advocates for dialogue and collaboration among scientists, ethicists, policymakers, and the wider community to ensure that ethical boundaries are respected and the dignity of creation is upheld.

Regulatory frameworks play a crucial role in aligning genetic interventions with ethical principles. The Church calls for stringent oversight mechanisms that evaluate genetic modification projects based on their environmental impact, potential health risks, and alignment with moral values. These frameworks should facilitate transparent scientific inquiry while ensuring that ethical considerations are integral to the decision-making process. The participation of a diverse range of voices, including those from religious traditions, in shaping these frameworks is essential for fostering a comprehensive understanding of the ethical dimensions of genetic engineering.

The precautionary principle, another key aspect of Catholic teaching, emphasizes a 'better safe than sorry' approach to genetic intervention. This principle advises caution in the absence of full scientific certainty about the outcomes of genetic modifications, advocating for erring on the side of protecting nature's integrity. It reflects a commitment to safeguarding creation against potentially irreversible damage, highlighting the need for thorough risk assessments and the development of safety measures before proceeding with genetic interventions.

Education and public engagement are also vital components of the Catholic approach to genetic engineering. By fostering a well-informed public discourse on the ethical implications of genetic interventions, the Church seeks to empower individuals and communities to participate actively in debates and decision-making processes. This engagement is crucial for cultivating a collective consciousness that values and defends the sanctity of creation.

Thus, the Catholic perspective on genetic intervention in nature is characterized by a dual commitment to embracing the potential of scientific advancements for the common good, while vigilantly safeguarding the integrity of creation. This delicate balance necessitates a discerning ethical framework, guided by principles of dignity, stewardship, and the common good. As humanity stands on the precipice of unparalleled technological capabilities, the wisdom of Catholic teaching offers an enduring moral compass, steering the course of genetic engineering towards a future that honors and preserves the natural world.

Ethical Considerations in Agricultural Biotechnology

In delving into the ethical implications of agricultural biotechnology, it's imperative to scrutinize the interconnectedness between human actions and their reverberations throughout the natural world. The discussion here is poised on the brink of a confluence between time-honored moral tradition and the burgeoning field of genetic engineering, specifically within the realm of agriculture. The dialogue entails not just an examination of the technology itself, but a profound contemplation of the values, objectives, and consequences that underpin its utilization.

At the core of agricultural biotechnology lies the manipulation of living organisms to enhance or modify their characteristics for human benefit. It's a practice that isn't new to humanity; however, the advent of sophisticated genetic technologies like CRISPR has escalated its possibilities and ethical stakes. One of the primary justifications for such genetic interventions in agriculture is the enhancement of food security. By modifying crops to increase their yield, resistance to pests and diseases, and tolerance to adverse climatic conditions, scientists aim to secure the food supply for a growing global population.

Yet, this pursuit of agricultural efficiency via genetic means raises a suite of ethical queries. Central to these concerns is the principle of respect for nature's intrinsic values. From a perspective that cherishes the sanctity of the natural order, any form of genetic manipulation must be approached with circumspection. It invites a critical inquiry into whether such practices uphold or erode the inherent dignity and worth embedded within the creation.

The commodification of life forms is yet another pressing ethical issue. By patenting genetically engineered seeds, biotechnology companies have turned these seeds into proprietary commodities. This commercialization strategy not only fosters economic dependencies but also raises questions about the ownership of life itself. It's a paradigm that challenges us to reconsider the moral ramifications of treating living entities as mere items for transaction.

Environmental concerns also loom large within this ethical landscape. The widespread adoption of genetically modified organisms (GMOs) in agriculture can lead to a reduction in biodiversity. This loss is not merely a biological issue but carries profound moral implications. Biodiversity is a testament to the richness of creation, and its diminution can be viewed as a contravention of our stewardship obligations to preserve and respect the natural world.

Equally, the potential for genetic flow between GMOs and non-GMOs poses risks of unforeseen consequences, such as the emergence of superweeds or the alteration of natural plant genomes. Such risks necessitate a precautionary approach, anchored in the moral principle of prudence. This principle admonishes that the potential long-term and irreversible impacts of genetic manipulation demand thorough scrutiny before embarking on widespread implementation.

Furthermore, the ethical discourse on agricultural biotechnology must consider social justice implications. The accessibility of genetically modified seeds is predominantly constrained to wealthier regions, exacerbating existing inequalities in global agriculture. This disparity constitutes a moral concern, highlighting the imperative to ensure that the benefits of biotechnological advancements are equitably distributed. Engaging with this technology ethically involves reflecting on how its applications might either alleviate or amplify social disparities.

The ethical deliberations surrounding agricultural biotechnology compel us to confront the foundational question of what it means to engage responsibly with the power of genetic engineering. It's a reflection that transcends mere cost-benefit analysis, urging a thoughtful integration of moral insights into the fabric of scientific innovation. The ethical framework within which such technologies are developed and applied bears significant weight on their legitimacy and societal acceptance.

In this contemplation, a balance must be sought. While acknowledging the potential of genetic engineering to address pressing agricultural challenges, the ethical approach requires a conscientious evaluation of the means employed and their congruence with commonly held moral values. It mandates a vigilance against reducing ethical considerations to mere technicalities, emphasizing instead a holistic view that places human dignity, respect for nature, and social justice at the forefront of innovation.

The deliberation on the ethical dimensions of agricultural biotechnology is not a conclusion but an ongoing dialogue. It's a discourse that necessitates the engagement of diverse voices from the scientific, ethical, and religious communities. This inclusive conversation aims not only to navigate the moral complexities but also to harness the collective wisdom in steering the application of genetic technologies towards the common good.

In summary, agricultural biotechnology presents a profound moral landscape, fraught with questions of respect for nature, the commodification of life, environmental sustainability, and social justice. It challenges us to ponder deeply about the kind of relationship humanity ought to foster with the natural world in the era of genetic engineering. Ethical engagement with agricultural biotechnology, therefore, becomes an imperative, guiding humanity in its stewardship of creation towards a future that cherishes life in all its forms.

Chapter 10: The Future of Genetics: Hope, Hype, and Humanity

The horizon of genetic engineering stretches far and wide, a testament to human curiosity and endeavor. Yet, as we peer into this expanse, we find ourselves caught between the polarities of hope and hype, both of which tug at the very fabric of our humanity. The future of genetics, while shimmering with promise, is fraught with ethical quandaries. As we navigate this terrain, imbued with the wisdom of Catholic teachings, we must discern the path that upholds the dignity of human life, the sanctity of creation, and the principles of justice and equity.

Hope is a fundamental tenet of the human condition, driving us toward betterment. In the realm of genetics, this hope is manifest in the potential to cure diseases, improve crop yields, and even extend human lifespan. However, this hope is not without its shadow, as the specter of hype often overpromises, underdelivers, and sometimes veils the ethical implications of such advancements. It's imperative that we temper our optimism with a critical lens, scrutinizing the moral dimensions of genetic technologies.

In examining the potentialities of genetic engineering, we must anchor our ethical considerations in the dignity of human life. This principle, central to Catholic bioethics, mandates that any genetic intervention must aim at the genuine wellbeing of the person, respecting their intrinsic value rather than treating them as means to an end. Herein lies a caution against technologies like CRISPR-Cas9, which, while offering significant medical breakthroughs, also pose profound ethical dilemmas regarding germline editing and the potential to engineer future generations (National Academy of Sciences, 2017).

The arena of gametogenesis and in vitro fertilization (IVF) further exemplifies the ethical tightrope in genetic science. While these technologies hold the promise of aiding couples struggling with infertility, they also raise imperative questions about the commodification of human life, the rights of the unborn, and the natural moral boundaries that might be crossed in the pursuit of conception (Congregation for the Doctrine of the Faith, 2008).

Eugenics and the prospect of designer babies represent another ethical frontier. The quest for perfection, driven by a flawed understanding of human worth, rekindles the eugenics debate, evoking memories of a dark past where the value of life was measured by arbitrary standards of fitness and desirability. Catholic ethics, with its emphasis on the immeasurable value of every human being, offers a robust counterpoint to this ideology, advocating for an unconditional respect for life that transcends genetic makeup.

As we contemplate the social ramifications of genetic engineering, the issue of equitable access emerges as a significant concern. The potential for life-saving therapies brings into sharp relief the disparities between the wealthy and the poor. Catholic social teaching, with its preferential option for the poor, challenges us to ensure that the benefits of genetic advancements don't become privileges for the few but instead serve the common good, especially the most vulnerable (Pope Francis, 2015).

In engaging with the environment, the application of genetic engineering in agriculture and conservation presents a dual-edged sword. On one hand, we find opportunities for sustainable development and the alleviation of hunger. On the other, we face ethical questions about our stewardship of creation and the respect owed to the natural order. Hence, ethical discernment must guide these endeavors, ensuring that our genetic interventions honor the integrity of creation rather than exploiting it.

The future of genetics, therefore, calls for a dialogue that bridges science and ethics, allowing for advancements that respect human dignity, promote justice, and preserve creation. This dialogue must be inclusive, engaging scientists, ethicists, faith leaders, and the wider community in a conversation that acknowledges the complexities and seeks a path forward that is both hopeful and ethically sound.

In conclusion, as we stand at the crossroads of hope and hype, the teachings and principles of Catholic ethics offer a guiding light. The future of genetics is not predetermined but is shaped by the choices we make today. Let us choose a future that respects the sanctity of life, embraces the common good, and upholds the dignity of all humanity.

Navigating Between Techno-Optimism and Bio-Pessimism

The conversation surrounding the future of genetics oscillates between two polar perspectives: techno-optimism, the belief in technology's potential to drastically improve the human condition, and bio-pessimism, the skepticism towards technological advancements due to ethical, social, and ecological concerns. This duality presents a challenging landscape for society, particularly from a Catholic ethical viewpoint, which seeks to mediate between these extremes with a principled yet compassionate approach.

Techno-optimism in the realm of genetics is fueled by the promise of technologies like CRISPR-Cas9, offering the tantalizing prospect of eradicating hereditary diseases, extending human life, and even enhancing human abilities. This optimistic outlook is rooted in a belief in human ingenuity's capacity to harness scientific advancements for the greater good. It echoes a deeply human desire for progress and perfection, traits which, when properly oriented, can indeed reflect the greater glory.

Conversely, bio-pessimism stems from legitimate concerns over the ethical ramifications of unchecked genetic manipulation. It invokes visions of a future where socio-economic disparities are exacerbated by access to genetic enhancements, where the sanctity of human life is compromised by eugenic practices, and where biodiversity is threatened by aggressive genetic interventions in nature. Such concerns resonate with the Catholic commitment to protect the vulnerable, preserve human dignity, and steward the creation responsibly.

From the Catholic perspective, navigating between these extremes requires a nuanced understanding of the moral principles guiding human action, particularly as they pertain to the sanctity of life, the dignity of the human person, and the common good. This necessitates a discerning engagement with the world of genetics, recognizing its potential for good while being critically aware of the moral pitfalls that accompany technological advances.

A key principle in this navigation is the inherent dignity of the human person, a concept that serves as a moral compass amidst the complexities of genetic technologies.

This dignity is not contingent upon one's genetic makeup or potential for enhancement but is an intrinsic aspect of being human, created in the image and likeness of God. Consequently, any genetic intervention must be evaluated in light of its respect for human dignity, ensuring that it neither commodifies human life nor diminishes its inherent worth.

The principle of the common good further informs the Catholic stance on genetic technologies. This principle advocates for a societal orientation toward the well-being of all, particularly the most vulnerable. In the context of genetics, this translates into advocating for equitable access to genetic therapies and cautioning against any form of genetic enhancement that could deepen social inequalities or foster new forms of discrimination.

Moral discernment in this field also involves grappling with the notion of natural law, which posits that moral principles are grounded in the very nature of humanity and the world. This framework challenges us to consider whether certain genetic interventions align with or diverge from the natural order and the purposes inscribed within it. Such reflection does not lead to a blanket rejection of genetic technologies but rather to a critical appraisal of their ethical implications.

Navigating between techno-optimism and bio-pessimism thus requires a delicate balance, one that embraces the potential of genetic technologies to alleviate suffering and enhance human life, while simultaneously guarding against the ethical perils they pose. This balance is not static but is constantly recalibrated in response to new scientific developments and evolving ethical insights.

In this journey, the Catholic ethical tradition offers a rich resource for reflection, providing principles that can guide humanity's engagement with genetic technologies. These principles do not offer easy answers but rather a framework for ongoing dialogue, discernment, and decision-making. They call us to a hopeful yet cautious approach, one that recognizes the potential of genetic technologies to contribute to human flourishing while remaining vigilant against their capacity to harm.

In conclusion, the future of genetics is fraught with both hope and hype, promise and peril. Navigating between techno-optimism and bio-pessimism demands a discerning ethical stance, one that is informed by deep respect for human dignity, commitment to the common good, and sensitivity to the moral dimensions of technological advancement. As we chart this course, the Catholic ethical tradition offers invaluable insights and principles to guide us, ensuring that our journey into the genetic future is marked by both ethical integrity and human compassion.

Catholic Insights into Hope and Caution for the Future

As we've journeyed together through the complex landscape of genetic technology, from the foundational principles of Catholic bioethics to the intricate dilemmas posed by CRISPR, gametogenesis, and in vitro fertilization, a tapestry of moral, ethical, and theological considerations has been woven. In this final analysis, it's paramount to draw upon the rich heritage of Catholic thought to discern a path forward that navigates both the hope and caution that characterize the future of genetics.

The hope is palpable. The potential of genetic technologies to cure diseases, to alleviate suffering, and to enhance the quality of human life aligns closely with the Catholic commitment to the sanctity of life and the call to care for the most vulnerable among us. And yet, this tide of optimism must be tempered by a sober caution, an acknowledgment of the ethical quagmires and the potential for harm that lie beneath the surface of these scientific advances.

The principle of the dignity of human life stands as a beacon of light guiding the Catholic approach to genetic engineering. This tenet, deeply embedded in Catholic teaching, asserts that every human being, from conception to natural death, possesses an intrinsic worth that demands respect and protection. The promise of genetic technologies to repair broken genes or to prevent hereditary diseases speaks to a profound hope that we can honor this dignity in new and profound ways. However, the caution comes in recognizing the delicate balance between therapeutic intervention and the potential for unintended consequences, including the slippery slope toward designing life in ways that might upend the natural order and devalue the very essence of human uniqueness.

The concept of natural law, a core element of Catholic moral theology, provides a foundation for evaluating the moral legitimacy of genetic interventions. Natural law teaches us that moral actions are those that align with the ultimate purposes or 'ends' inscribed in the natural order of creation. Therefore, genetic interventions aimed at healing and restoring the natural functioning of the human body can be seen as morally licit. But where genetic manipulation seeks to 'improve' or alter human nature beyond its natural limits, we encounter moral peril.

The principle of double effect, another critical tool in Catholic ethical reasoning, helps to disentangle the knotty problems of interventions that could have both positive and negative outcomes. This principle allows for actions that have an intended good effect, even if they risk a potential harm, provided the action itself is not intrinsically evil, and the good effect is not achieved through bad means. Applying this principle to genetic engineering demands a careful consideration of both the intended aims and the potential collateral consequences of genetic interventions.

In confronting the challenges of genetic engineering, the Catholic tradition brings a message of hope grounded in the belief in human creativity as a reflection of the Creator's own ingenuity. This optimistic view encourages the pursuit of scientific advancements that can alleviate human suffering and improve the human condition. However, this hope is not naïve. It is balanced by a keen awareness of the fallibility of human endeavors and the need for ethical guidelines that safeguard against hubris and exploitation.

As we look to the future, the preferential option for the poor, a principle that prioritizes the needs of the most vulnerable in society, becomes particularly relevant in the context of genetic technologies. The hope for genetic therapies and interventions that can transform lives must be accompanied by a caution against creating a new form of inequality, where only the wealthy have access to these life-altering advances. Catholic social teaching thus demands that we consider the common good, ensuring that the benefits of genetic engineering are accessible to all, particularly those who are most in need.

The potential environmental impact of genetic manipulation, especially in agriculture, also warrants careful consideration from a Catholic perspective. The stewardship of creation, a responsibility entrusted to humanity by the Creator, requires that we approach genetic interventions in nature with humility and caution, balancing the hope for increased food production and disease resistance with the imperative to protect the integrity and diversity of the created world.

As genetic technologies continue to evolve, the Catholic Church calls for ongoing dialogue between scientists, ethicists, theologians, and the wider community. This collaborative approach aims to foster a culture of ethical reflection that can discern wisely between beneficial advancements and ethically problematic applications. It is in this dialogue that the Church hopes to contribute its insights into human dignity, natural law, and the common good, shaping a future in which genetic technologies serve to enhance human life without compromising moral values.

In conclusion, the Catholic insights into hope and caution for the future of genetic technologies offer a balanced perspective that celebrates the potential for scientific progress while steadfastly upholding ethical principles. As we embrace the possibilities that lie on the horizon, let us move forward with a critical awareness, guided by a moral compass grounded in a deep respect for the dignity of all life, a commitment to the common good, and a love for the natural order that reflects the wisdom of the Creator.

Embracing the Future with Ethical Integrity

As we stand at the threshold of significant advancements in genetic technologies, the imperative for ethical integrity has never been more critical. The convergence of groundbreaking scientific discoveries with profound ethical considerations presents a unique challenge to the Roman Catholic community, ethicists, and university professors alike. The promise and peril of such technologies, including CRISPR-Cas9, gametogenesis, and in vitro fertilization (IVF), necessitate a robust moral framework rooted in the enduring principles of Catholic bioethics.

In the endeavor to articulate a response to these burgeoning technologies, it is essential to foreground the sanctity of life, a cornerstone of Catholic teaching. This precept, while seemingly straightforward, assumes profound complexities in the context of genetic manipulation, where the potential to alter the essence of life itself stands at our fingertips. By adhering to the principle of the dignity of every human life, we form the bedrock upon which all subsequent ethical deliberations must rest.

Among the constellation of ethical concerns, CRISPR-Cas9 technology epitomizes the profound dualities of genetic engineering. While it heralds unprecedented opportunities for eradicating genetic diseases, it simultaneously beckons the specter of eugenics and designer babies. In navigating this dichotomy, the application of Catholic moral principles, particularly the principle of double effect, becomes instrumental. This principle allows for the consideration of actions that may produce both good and evil effects, thereby guiding ethically permissible interventions under stringent conditions.

Similarly, the advent of gametogenesis and IVF technologies propels us into uncharted ethical territories. These methods, while offering hope to countless couples grappling with infertility, also pose salient challenges to the traditional Catholic doctrines concerning procreation and the sanctity of life from conception. In contemplating these technologies, the moral compass of the Church calls for a discernment that encompasses both compassion for human suffering and fidelity to doctrinal teachings.

The discourse on the ethical implications of genetic engineering cannot be confined to abstract theological or philosophical considerations. Rather, it must engage with the lived realities of individuals and societies. The evolution of genetic technologies undeniably holds the promise of revolutionizing healthcare, potentially eradicating genetic disorders that have plagued humanity for centuries. However, this revolution carries with it questions of justice, particularly the equitable access to genetic therapies across socioeconomic divides.

The preferential option for the poor, a principle deeply embedded in Catholic social teaching, mandates a critical examination of the accessibility of genetic treatments. The potential for these technologies to exacerbate existing inequalities demands a concerted effort to ensure that the fruits of genetic research benefit all of humanity, not merely the privileged few.

Moreover, the stewardship of creation compels us to consider the ramifications of genetic interventions in the natural world. The manipulation of genetic material in agriculture, while promising enhanced food security and sustainability, warrants a cautious approach rooted in respect for the integrity of creation.

The ethical landscape of genetic engineering is fraught with dilemmas that defy simple resolutions. In addressing these challenges, the Roman Catholic tradition offers a wealth of moral resources. The synthesis of reason and faith, characteristic of Catholic ethical reflection, provides a comprehensive framework for navigating the moral quandaries presented by genetic technologies.

However, the pursuit of ethical integrity in the context of genetic engineering is not a solitary endeavor reserved for theologians and ethicists. It demands a collaborative dialogue that bridges ecclesial, scientific, and societal realms. By fostering a discourse that is inclusive, informed, and reflective, we can aspire to a future where genetic technologies are wielded with wisdom, compassion, and an unwavering commitment to the common good.

This journey towards embracing the future with ethical integrity is a testament to the enduring relevance of Catholic bioethical principles in addressing the complex moral issues of our time. By grounding our responses in the sanctity of life, the dignity of the human person, and a preferential option for the poor, we endeavor to navigate the ethical frontiers of genetic technologies with discernment and fidelity to our moral heritage.

As we advance into this uncharted territory, let us be guided by a hope that is both cautious and courageous. The future of genetic engineering, with all its promises and challenges, beckons us to engage with it thoughtfully and ethically. In doing so, we affirm our commitment to nurturing a society that respects the inherent dignity of all life and seeks the flourishing of every human person.

In conclusion, the moral discourse surrounding genetic technologies is emblematic of the broader ethical challenges facing humanity in the 21st century. By embracing the future with ethical integrity, rooted in the rich tradition of Catholic bioethics, we can contribute to the shaping of a world marked by justice, compassion, and respect for the sanctity of life. It is a journey fraught with uncertainties, but also abounding with hope. For in the quest to navigate the moral complexities of genetic engineering, we are called not only to safeguard the integrity of life but also to envision a future where technology serves the common good of all.

Glossary of Terms in Catholic Bioethics and Genetic Technology

As we delve into the complexities and moral challenges posed by advances in genetic technology, a clear understanding of specific terms and concepts is essential for meaningful discourse. This glossary aims to equip readers with a foundational comprehension of critical terms used throughout discussions on Catholic bioethics and genetic technology.

CRISPR-Cas9

A revolutionary genetic editing technology that allows for precise, directed changes to genomic DNA. CRISPR-Cas9 has been hailed for its potential to correct genetic defects and treat hereditary diseases but raises ethical concerns, especially regarding germline editing and potential unintended consequences (Doudna & Charpentier, 2016).

Double Effect, Principle of

A moral principle in Catholic ethics that allows an action that causes a serious harm as a side effect of promoting some good end, under specific conditions. It is particularly pertinent in medical ethics, where treatments may have harmful side effects (Kohlhaas, 2021).

Eugenics

The practice or advocacy of improving the genetic quality of the human population, often by excluding certain genetic groups or characteristics deemed undesirable. The Catholic Church opposes eugenics as it fundamentally disrespects the dignity of human life and can lead to discrimination and social injustices (Paul II, 1995).

Gametogenesis

An artificial process of generating gametes—human sperm or eggs—outside the body from stem cells. While it holds promise for addressing infertility, it also presents ethical dilemmas, particularly concerning the manipulation of human life at its earliest stages (ant, 2017).

Genetic Engineering

The direct manipulation of an organism's genes using biotechnology. It encompasses a range of techniques, including genetic modification and gene editing. The Catholic ethical perspective critiques its applications based on their respect for human dignity and the natural order.

In Vitro Fertilization (IVF)

A medical procedure whereby an egg is fertilized by sperm in a test tube or elsewhere outside the body. The Catholic Church raises moral objections to IVF on several grounds, including the sanctity of marriage and the belief that life begins at conception (Congregation for the Doctrine of the Faith, 1987).

Natural Law

A theory asserting that certain rights or values are inherent by virtue of human nature and universally cognizable through human reason. Catholic bioethics draws heavily on natural law theory, seeing it as foundational for moral decision-making (ant, 2017).

Sanctity of Life

A principle asserting that all human life is inherently valuable and deserving of respect from conception until natural death. This concept is central to Catholic teaching on bioethics, informing the Church's stance on issues like abortion, euthanasia, and genetic engineering.

Throughout this text, these terms and concepts weave together to present a Catholic ethical perspective on the moral challenges posed by genetic technology. By understanding these foundational elements, readers are better equipped to engage with the nuanced ethical discussions these advances elicit.

Appendix A: Church Documents on Bioethics and Genetic Engineering

The field of bioethics, particularly genetic engineering, confronts humanity with profound moral implications. It calls for a discerning and ethically rigorous approach, especially from a Roman Catholic perspective. Genetic interventions, including CRISPR-Cas9 technology, gametogenesis, and in vitro fertilization (IVF), present not merely scientific advancements but also deep ethical quandaries that touch the very essence of human dignity and the sanctity of life.

At the heart of Catholic bioethical considerations is the intrinsic dignity of every human being. This foundational principle is grounded in the belief that every person is created in the image and likeness of God. Thus, human life is inviolable from conception until natural death. This belief underpins the Church's approach to bioethical issues, where the sanctity of life and the integrity of the natural procreative process are paramount.

In facing the challenges posed by genetic engineering, the Catholic Church has not remained silent. Various documents have been promulgated by the Magisterium – the teaching authority of the Church – to provide guidance and articulate the Church's stance on these critical moral issues. These documents serve as a beacon of light, guiding the faithful through the murky waters of modern bioethical dilemmas.

One pivotal document is "Dignitas Personae" (The Dignity of a Person), issued by the Congregation for the Doctrine of the Faith in 2008. This instruction provides explicit moral guidance on bioethical issues, emphasizing that human life is sacred and deserving of respect at all stages of development. It addresses specific practices like IVF, stem cell research, and genetic manipulation, underscoring the moral dangers inherent in treating human life as a mere means to an end.

"Donum Vitae" (The Gift of Life), published in 1987 by the same Congregation, precedes "Dignitas Personae" and lays the groundwork for the Church's teaching on the respect due to human embryos. It examines the ethical implications of biotechnological advancements in human procreation, strongly advocating for the transmission of life to be rooted in the marital act—a position further iterated and expanded upon in "Dignitas Personae".

Furthermore, the encyclical "Evangelium Vitae" (The Gospel of Life) promulgated by St. John Paul II in 1995, serves as a comprehensive declaration on the value and inviolability of human life. While it primarily addresses issues like abortion and euthanasia, its underlying principles are profoundly relevant to the ethical evaluation of genetic engineering and biotechnology practices. It reinforces the notion that every human being is a unique and unrepeatable gift, with an inherent right to life.

Additionally, the Pontifical Academy for Life, established in 1994, has been instrumental in articulating the Church's ethical positions in the burgeoning field of biotechnology. Through its various publications and statements, the Academy has contributed significantly to the discourse on the moral implications of genetic engineering, seeking to harmonize scientific progress with the ethical demands of human dignity.

While these documents form the core of the Church's teachings on bioethics and genetic engineering, they are part of a broader tradition of Catholic moral theology. This tradition seeks to engage with contemporary challenges in a manner that is both intellectually rigorous and faith-filled. It invites dialogue with the scientific community, proposing a holistic understanding of the human person that encompasses both the material and spiritual dimensions of existence.

The Church's teachings on bioethics and genetic engineering do not merely impose restrictions but aim to foster an ethical culture that promotes genuine human flourishing. They challenge society to ponder the deeper meaning of progress and to consider the ethical boundaries that should guide scientific exploration. In doing so, they call for a technological development that is not disconnected from moral principles but is instead informed by a profound respect for human dignity and the common good.

As we venture further into the realm of genetic engineering, the wisdom contained in these Church documents remains ever relevant. They provide ethical signposts that help navigate the complex moral landscape of modern biotechnological advancements. By engaging with these teachings, the faithful are equipped to face these challenges with moral clarity and an unwavering commitment to the protection of human dignity.

Indeed, the ongoing dialogue between faith and reason, as extolled by the Catholic intellectual tradition, is indispensable in addressing the ethical dilemmas posed by genetic engineering. It is through this dialogue that a path can be charted towards a future where scientific progress serves the true good of humanity, reflecting the Creator's love and the intrinsic worth of every human being.

In conclusion, the Church's documents on bioethics and genetic engineering are invaluable resources for all who seek to explore the ethical implications of genetic technologies within the framework of Catholic moral teaching. They challenge us to ponder not just what can be done, but what ought to be done, in pursuit of a world that fully honors the gift of life and the human person's transcendent dignity.

Appendix B: Further Reading and Resources

The progression of genetic engineering technologies, including CRISPR, gametogenesis, and in vitro fertilization (IVF), presents complex moral dilemmas that demand careful consideration and a deep understanding of both the scientific intricacies and the ethical principles involved. As a continuation of our exploration into these issues through the lens of Catholic bioethics, this appendix aims to provide a vast array of resources for further reading. These include theological discourses, scientific studies, philosophical works, and more, each contributing to a nuanced understanding of the implications of genetic engineering within the realm of Catholic ethical thought.

In addressing the ethical considerations of CRISPR technology, one must delve into the scientific fundamentals that underpin gene editing, as well as the moral implications of altering genetic material. A seminal resource in this area is "CRISPR-Cas: A Laboratory Manual" (Doudna & Charpentier, 2016), which offers an exhaustive overview of CRISPR technology from a scientific perspective. Complementing this, "Gene Editing: Scientific Opportunities, Public Interests, and Policy

Options in the Developing World" (Parrington, 2016) explores the global implications of gene editing, providing a balanced view between the potential benefits and ethical concerns, particularly in relation to social justice issues.

For those interested in the Catholic Church's stance on gametogenesis, "The Ethics of Human Artificial Gametes" (Flaman, 2002) provides a comprehensive examination of the moral and ethical debates surrounding the creation of artificial gametes. This work, while not exclusively from a Catholic viewpoint, offers critical insights that can inform a Catholic ethical perspective.

The moral examination of in vitro fertilization (IVF) from a Catholic perspective necessitates an understanding of the Church's teachings on the sanctity of life and the marital act. "Begotten Not Made: A Catholic View of Reproductive Technology" (Congregation for the Doctrine of the Faith, 2008) elaborates on the Church's position regarding IVF and other reproductive technologies, highlighting the moral issues associated with IVF, including the disposal of embryos and the separation of procreation from the conjugal act.

The discourse on eugenics and designer babies within Catholic bioethics is enriched by a historical understanding of eugenics movements and their ethical implications. "Eugenics and the Ethics of Selective Reproduction" (Kohlhaas, 2021) examines the ethical fallacies of the quest for human perfection through selective reproduction, offering insights into the dangers of eugenic ideologies.

In considering the sanctity of life within the context of genetic manipulation, "The Immoral Situation of Abortion and In Vitro Fertilization: Issues Concerning the Family and the Paradox of Fertility" (ant, 2017) critically assesses how biotechnological advances challenge our understanding of human dignity and vulnerability. This work sparks reflection on preserving human dignity amidst the advancement of genetic engineering.

The challenge of ensuring equitable access to genetic therapies is a pressing social justice issue within Catholic social teaching. "Justice and the Human Genome Project" (Murray, 1994) confronts the disparities in accessing genetic medicine, urging a preferential option for the poor in the distribution of genetic therapies.

Modifying creation through genetic intervention in nature mandates a careful ethical consideration of our stewardship over the environment. "Genetic Technology and Environmental Ethics" (Flaman, 2002) delves into the Catholic perspectives on environmental intervention, offering a thoughtful exploration of the Church's teachings on creation and our responsibility towards it.

Lastly, looking towards the future of genetics with hope and caution requires a balanced perspective grounded in ethical integrity. "The Ethics of Genetic Engineering" (Meilaender, 2013) offers Catholic insights into navigating the promises and perils of genetic technologies, advocating for a future where technology serves humanity's genuine well-being without compromising moral principles.

These resources, while providing a foundation for further exploration, represent only a fraction of the vast literature available on the ethics of genetic engineering through a Catholic lens. They serve as a starting point for those seeking to deepen their understanding of these complex moral issues.

Chapter 11: Bibliography

In our exploration of the complex interface between Catholic ethics and the rapid advancements in genetic technologies, we have traversed from the foundational principles of moral theology to the forefront of genetic manipulation and beyond. This bibliography, therefore, serves not merely as a catalog of sources but as a testament to the breadth and depth of scholarship that has informed our discourse. The references contained within this chapter are curated to provide a comprehensive and critical foundation for further inquiry into the ethical dimensions of genetic engineering from a Catholic perspective.

The ethical considerations surrounding CRISPR technology and its implications for the sanctity of human life are discussed extensively in the literature. Among these, the works of (Doudna & Charpentier, 2016), offer a compelling analysis of CRISPR's ethical landscape juxtaposing its scientific promise against the moral perils that lurk beneath its surface.

Focusing on in vitro fertilization (IVF), the scholarship of Dr. ant (2017) sheds light on the moral quandaries inherent in these reproductive technologies. Their research critically examines IVF through the prism of Catholic moral teaching, unraveling the complex ethical issues that accompany the manipulation of human life at its very inception.

When addressing the topic of genetic gametogenesis, the pioneering work of Kohlhass (2021) provides invaluable insights into the ethical challenges posed by the creation of gametes in a laboratory setting. His comprehensive review delineates the fine ethical lines that these technologies tread, offering a nuanced perspective that is deeply rooted in the principles of Catholic bioethics.

The moral evils of eugenics and the pursuit of 'designer babies' are critically analyzed through the lens of Catholic ethics in the groundbreaking studies by Flaman (2002). He offers an in-depth exploration of the ethical fallacies that underpin the eugenic mindset, drawing upon Catholic teaching to mount a vigorous defense of the inviolable dignity of human life.

In the realm of healthcare, genetics, and their implications for the poor, the work of Parrington (2016) stands out for its thorough examination of the social justice issues entangled with genetic therapies. His research critically evaluates the unequal access to genetic medicine and its impact on marginalized communities, guided by the Catholic preferential option for the poor.

Also, the environmental consequences of genetic engineering are meticulously explored by Flaman (2002), who delve into the ethical considerations surrounding genetic interventions in nature. His analysis, framed within Catholic perspectives on stewardship and creation, provides a thoughtful examination of the moral dimensions of agricultural biotechnology.

Looking toward the future of genetics, the optimistic and pessimistic visions of biotechnological progress are balanced in the reflections offered by Carter et al. (2023). Their work encapsulates the Catholic insights into the dual nature of hope and caution that characterizes the ethical approach to emerging genetic technologies.

Each of these contributions enriches our understanding of the profound ethical challenges and considerations that Catholic moral theology must address in the context of modern genetic technologies. The dialogue between faith and science, as illuminated by these works, underscores the necessity of an informed and conscientious engagement with the moral dilemmas of our time.

As we contemplate the future of genetics, may this bibliography serve as a beacon that guides us toward ethical integrity, informed by the rich tapestry of Catholic moral teaching and the perennial quest for truth and virtue in the face of scientific advancement.

It is our hope that the scholarship cited herein will inspire further inquiry and dialogue, fostering a deeper comprehension of the moral imperatives that guide our ethical navigation of the genetic frontier. May the exploration of these references enrich your understanding and spur you toward thoughtful engagement with the ethical challenges of our contemporary world.

In closing, this bibliography is offered as a resource for all who seek to grapple with the complex ethical issues at the intersection of Catholic teaching and genetic engineering. Let it be a starting point for a journey of intellectual discovery and moral discernment, one that contributes to the flourishing of human dignity and the common good in the age of biotechnological innovation.

Chapter 12: Acknowledgments

The journey through the complex terrain of genetic engineering and Catholic bioethics would have been insurmountable without the support and wisdom of many individuals and institutions. In recognizing their invaluable contributions, it is with profound gratitude that this chapter is dedicated to acknowledging their efforts.

Firstly, the grounding in Catholic bioethics that this work attempts to navigate owes a substantial debt to the numerous theologians and ethicists whose teachings and writings have illuminated the path. While their insights have been instrumental in shaping the discussions herein, it is the spirit of intellectual inquiry they champion that has truly guided this exploration.

The scientific community's relentless pursuit of knowledge, especially those dedicated to the advancements in genetic engineering, has provided the foundation upon which this text's discussions are built. Their commitment to unraveling the mysteries of life at the genetic level has not only propelled humanity forward but has also presented the ethical dilemmas this book seeks to address.

Sincere appreciation is also due to the Roman Catholic Church, whose teachings and documents have been a constant source of wisdom and guidance. The Church's engagement with the questions posed by modern science and technology has been an invaluable resource in understanding the ethical dimensions of these issues.

To the librarians and staff at the institutions that have provided access to their resources and collections, your assistance has been a cornerstone in the construction of this work. The ability to delve into the vast repositories of knowledge you maintain has been a privilege.

To my readers, for engaging with this work and considering its perspectives, I am deeply grateful. It is my hope that it contributes in some way to the ongoing dialogue between faith and science, and aids in navigating the ethical complexities of our genetic future with integrity and wisdom.

As we stand at the crossroads of genetic discovery and ethical reflection, may we continue to seek wisdom, foster dialogue, and uphold the dignity of all life in our shared pursuit of truth.

References

1. Catholic Health Association of the United States. (2019). Health care and genetic technology: Balancing innovation and the common good.

2. National Institutes of Health. (2021). Gene therapy and genetic research for sickle cell disease.

3. World Health Organization. (2022). Sickle cell disease.

4. American Society for Reproductive Medicine. (2016). Ethical considerations for assisted reproductive technologies. Birmingham, AL: ASRM Ethics Committee.

5. Ijaz, S., Ul Haq, I. (2019). Recombinant DNA Technology. United Kingdom: Cambridge Scholars Publishing.

6. Catechism of the Catholic Church. (1997). 2nd ed. Washington, DC: United States Catholic Conference.

7. Church Document on Bioethics. (n.d.). Vatican City: Vatican Press.

8. Congregation for the Doctrine of the Faith. (2020). Dignitas Personae: On Certain Bioethical Questions. Vatican.

9. Church, G. M., & Regis, E. (2017). Regenesis: How synthetic biology will reinvent nature and ourselves. Basic Books.

10. Churchland, P.S. (2011). Braintrust: What Neuroscience Tells Us about Morality. Princeton University Press.

11. ant, Dr. (2017). The Immoral Situation of Abortion and In Vitro Fertilization: Issues Concerning the Family and the Paradox of Fertility. West Chester, PA: Saint Norbert Media, Inc.

12. ant, Dr. (2022). The philosophy of divine mercy. West Chester, PA: Saint Norbert Media, Inc.

13. Congregation for the Doctrine of the Faith. (1987). Donum Vitae. Vatican City: Vatican Press.

14. Congregation for the Doctrine of the Faith. (2008). Dignitas personae. Vatican City: Libreria Editrice Vaticana.

15. Doudna, J. A., & Charpentier, E. (2016). CRISPR-Cas: A Laboratory Manual. Cold Spring Harbor Laboratory Press. Woodbury, NY.

16. Evans, J. H. (2019). Playing God? Human Genetic Engineering and the Rationalization of Public Bioethical Debate. Chicago, IL: University of Chicago Press.

17. Greely, H. (2016). The End of Sex and the Future of Human Reproduction. Harvard University Press.

18. Henig, R. M. (2000). The Monk in the Garden: The Lost and Found Genius of Gregor Mendel, the Father of Genetics. Houghton Mifflin Harcourt.

19. Flaman, P. (2002). Genetic Engineering: Christian Values and Catholic Teaching. United States: Paulist Press.

20. John Paul II. (1995). Evangelium Vitae. Vatican City: Vatican Press.

21. Parrington, J. (2016). Redesigning Life: How Genome Editing Will Transform the World. United Kingdom: Oxford University Press.

22. McGonigle, I. V., Muthuswamy, V., & Kumar, N. K. (2022). Bridging the gap: Health equity and genetic medicine. Journal of Global Health, 12, 05001.

23. McKenny, G. (1997). To Relieve the Human Condition: Bioethics, Technology, and the Body. State University of New York Press.

24. Meilaender, G. (2013). Bioethics: A Primer for Christians. William B. Eerdmans Publishing Company.

25. Mendel, G. (1866). Experiments in plant hybridization. Proceedings of the Natural History Society of Brünn, IV.

26. Murray, T. H. (1994). Justice and the Human Genome Project. University of California Press.

27. National Academies of Sciences, Engineering, and Medicine. (2017). Human Genome Editing: Science, Ethics, and Governance. The National Academies Press.

28. National Catholic Bioethics Center. (n.d.). Catholic Teachings on IVF and Reproductive Technology. Retrieved from https://www.ncbcenter.org

29. John Paul II. (1995). Evangelium Vitae. Vatican: Libreria Editrice Vaticana.

30. Pontifical Academy for Life. (2023). Ethical considerations regarding new gene editing technologies. Vatican City: Libreria Editrice Vaticana.

31. Pope Francis. (2015). Laudato si' [Encyclical]. Vatican City: Libreria Editrice Vaticana.

32. Pope Paul VI Institute. (2023). Ethical Considerations on In Vitro Fertilization.

33. Kohlhaas, J. M. (2021). Beyond Biology: Rethinking Parenthood in the Catholic Tradition. United States: Georgetown University Press.

34. Sandel, M.J. (2007). The Case Against Perfection: Ethics in the Age of Genetic Engineering. Harvard University Press.

35. Shiva, V. (1997). Biopiracy: The plunder of nature and knowledge. South End Press.

36. Singer, P., & Mason, J. (2006). The ethics of what we eat: Why our food choices matter. Rodale.

37. Sulmasy, D. P. (2013). A Balm for Gilead: Meditations on Spirituality and the Healing Arts. Georgetown University Press.

38. United States Conference of Catholic Bishops. (2008). Forming consciences for faithful citizenship: A call to political responsibility from the Catholic bishops of the United States. Washington, D.C.: United States Conference of Catholic Bishops.

39. Vatican Dicastery for Life. (2020). Catholic Church Teaching on Bioethics and Human Dignity. Vatican City: Libreria Editrice Vaticana.

40. Watson, J. D. (1968). The Double Helix: A Personal Account of the Discovery of the Structure of DNA. Atheneum.

THE 15 PRAYERS OF ST. BRIDGET

These Prayers and these Promises have been copied from a book printed in Toulouse in 1740 and published by the P. Adrien Parvilliers of the Company of Jesus, Apostolic Missionary of the Holy Land, with approbation, permission and recommendation to distribute them.
Pope Pius IX took cognisance of these Prayers with the prologue; he approved them May 31, 1862, recognising them as true and for the good of souls.

As St. Bridget for a long time wanted to know the number of blows Our Lord received during His Passion, He one day appeared to her and said: "I received 5480 blows on My Body. If you wish to honour them in some way, say 15 Our Fathers and 15 Hail Marys with the following Prayers (which He taught her) for a whole year. When the year is up, you will have honoured each one of My Wounds."

He made the following promises to anyone who recited these Prayers for a whole year:

1. I will deliver 15 souls of his lineage from Purgatory.

2. 15 souls of his lineage will be confirmed and preserved in grace.

3. 15 sinners of his lineage will be converted.

4. Whoever recites these Prayers will attain the first degree of perfection.

5. 15 days before his death I will give him My Precious Body in order that he may escape eternal starvation; I will give him My Precious Blood to drink lest he thirst eternally.

6. 15 days before his death he will feel a deep contrition for all his sins and will have a perfect knowledge of them.

7. I will place before him the sign of My Victorious Cross for his help and defence against the attacks of his enemies.

8. Before his death I shall come with My Dearest Beloved Mother.

9. I shall graciously receive his soul, and will lead it into eternal joys.

10. And having led it there I shall give him a special draught from the fountain of My Deity, something I will not for those who have not recited My Prayers.

11. Let it be known that whoever may have been living in a state of mortal sin for 30 years, but who will recite devoutly, or have the intention to recite these Prayers, the Lord will forgive him all his sins.

12. I shall protect him from strong temptations.

13. I shall preserve and guard his 5 senses.

14. I shall preserve him from a sudden death.

15. His soul will be delivered from eternal death.

16. He will obtain all he asks for from God and the Blessed Virgin.

17. If he has lived all his life doing his own will and he is to die the next day, his life will be prolonged.

18. Every time one recites these Prayers he gains 100 days indulgence.

19. He is assured of being joined to the supreme Choir of Angels.

20. Whoever teaches these Prayers to another, will have continuous joy and merit which will endure eternally.

21. There where these Prayers are being said or will be said in the future God is present with His grace.

Each prayer is preceded by one Our Father and one Hail Mary.

Our Father, who art in heaven, hallowed be thy name.
Thy kingdom come.
Thy will be done on earth as it is in heaven.
Give us this day our daily bread and forgive us our trespasses as we forgive those who trespass against us and lead us not into temptation but deliver us from evil. **Amen**

Hail Mary, full of grace, the Lord is with thee; blessed art thou among women and blessed is the fruit of thy womb, Jesus.
Holy Mary, Mother of God, pray for us sinners, now and at the hour of our death. **Amen.**

FIRST PRAYER
Our Father – Hail Mary.
O Jesus Christ! Eternal Sweetness to those who love Thee, joy surpassing all joy and all desire, Salvation and Hope of all sinners, Who hast proved that Thou hast no greater desire than to be among men, even assuming human nature at the fullness of time for the love of men, recall all the sufferings Thou hast endured

from the instant of Thy conception, and especially during Thy Passion, as it was decreed and ordained from all eternity in the Divine plan.

Remember, O Lord, that during the Last Supper with Thy disciples, having washed their feet, Thou gavest them Thy Most Precious Body and Blood, and while at the same time thou didst sweetly console them, Thou didst foretell them Thy coming Passion.
Remember the sadness and bitterness which Thou didst experience in Thy Soul as Thou Thyself bore witness saying: "My Soul is sorrowful even unto death."

Remember all the fear, anguish and pain that Thou didst suffer in Thy delicate Body before the torment of the Crucifixion, when, after having prayed three times, bathed in a sweat of blood, Thou wast betrayed by Judas, Thy disciple, arrested by the people of a nation Thou hadst chosen and elevated, accused by false witnesses, unjustly judged by three judges during the flower of Thy youth and during the solemn Paschal season.

Remember that Thou wast despoiled of Thy garments and clothed in those of derision; that Thy Face and Eyes were veiled, that Thou wast buffeted, crowned with thorns, a reed placed in Thy Hands, that Thou was crushed with blows and overwhelmed with affronts and outrages.

In memory of all these pains and sufferings which Thou didst endure before Thy Passion on the Cross, grant me before my death true contrition, a sincere and entire confession, worthy satisfaction and the remission of all my sins. **Amen.**

SECOND PRAYER

Our Father – Hail Mary.

O Jesus! True liberty of angels, Paradise of delights, remember the horror and sadness which Thou didst endure when Thy enemies, like furious lions, surrounded Thee, and by thousands of insults, spits, blows, lacerations and other unheard-of-cruelties, tormented Thee at will.

In consideration of these torments and insulting words, I beseech Thee, O my Saviour, to deliver me from all my enemies, visible and invisible, and to bring me, under Thy protection, to the perfection of eternal salvation. **Amen.**

THIRD PRAYER
Our Father – Hail Mary.
O Jesus! Creator of Heaven and earth Whom nothing can encompass or limit, Thou Who dost enfold and hold all under Thy Loving power, remember the very bitter pain.

Thou didst suffer when the Jews nailed Thy Sacred Hands and Feet to the Cross by blow after blow with big blunt nails, and not finding Thee in a pitiable enough state to satisfy their rage, they enlarged Thy Wounds, and added pain to pain, and with indescribable cruelty stretched Thy Body on the Cross, pulled Thee from all sides, thus dislocating Thy Limbs.

I beg of Thee, O Jesus, by the memory of this most Loving suffering of the Cross, to grant me the grace to fear Thee and to Love Thee. **Amen.**

FOURTH PRAYER
Our Father - Hail Mary.

O Jesus! Heavenly Physician, raised aloft on the Cross to heal our wounds with Thine, remember the bruises which Thou didst suffer and the weakness of all Thy Members which were distended to such a degree that never was there pain like unto Thine.

From the crown of Thy Head to the Soles of Thy Feet there was not one spot on Thy Body that was not in torment, and yet, forgetting all Thy sufferings, Thou didst not cease to pray to Thy Heavenly Father for Thy enemies, saying: "Father forgive them for they know not what they do."

Through this great Mercy, and in memory of this suffering, grant that the remembrance of Thy Most Bitter Passion may effect in us a perfect contrition and the remission of all our sins. **Amen**.

FIFTH PRAYER

Our Father – Hail Mary.

O Jesus! Mirror of eternal splendour, remember the sadness which Thou experienced, when contemplating in the light of Thy Divinity the predestination of those who would be saved by the merits of Thy Sacred Passion.

Thou didst see at the same time, the great multitude of reprobates who would be damned for their sins, and Thou didst complain bitterly of those hopeless lost and unfortunate sinners.

Through this abyss of compassion and pity, and especially through the goodness which Thou displayed to the good thief when Thou saidst to him: "This day, thou shalt be with Me in Paradise." I beg of Thee, O Sweet Jesus, that at the hour of my death, Thou wilt show me mercy. **Amen**.

SIXTH PRAYER

Our Father – Hail Mary.

O Jesus! Beloved and most desirable King, remember the grief Thou didst suffer, when naked and like a common criminal.

Thou was fastened and raised on the Cross, when all Thy relatives and friends abandoned Thee, except Thy Beloved Mother, who remained close to Thee during Thy agony and whom Thou didst entrust to Thy faithful disciple when Thou saidst to Mary: "Woman, behold thy son!" and to St. John: "Son, behold thy Mother!"

I beg of Thee O my Saviour, by the sword of sorrow whlch pierced the soul of Thy holy Mother, to have compassion on me in all my affliction and tribulations, both corporal and spiritual, and to assist me in all my trials, and especially at the hour of my death. **Amen**.

SEVENTH PRAYER

Our Father – Hail Mary.

O Jesus! Inexhaustible Fountain of compassion, Who by a profound gesture of Love, said from the Cross: "I thirst!" suffered from the thirst for the salvation of the human race.

I beg of Thee O my Saviour, to inflame in our hearts the desire to tend toward perfection in all our acts; and to extinguish in us the concupiscence of the flesh and the ardor of worldly desires. **Amen**.

EIGHTH PRAYER

Our Father – Hail Mary.

O Jesus! Sweetness of hearts, delight of the spirit, by the bitterness of the vinegar and gall which Thou didst taste on the Cross for Love of us, grant us the grace to receive worthily.

Thy Precious Body and Blood during our life and at the hour of our death, that they may serve as a remedy and consolation for our souls. **Amen.**

NINTH PRAYER

Our Father – Hail Mary.

O Jesus! Royal virtue, joy of the mind, recall the pain
Thou didst endure when, plunged in an ocean of
bitterness at the approach of death, insulted, outraged
by the Jews.

Thou didst cry out in a loud voice that Thou was
abandoned by Thy Father, saying: "My God, My God,
why hast Thou forsaken me?"

Through this anguish, I beg of Thee, O my Saviour, not
to abandon me in the terrors and pains of my
death. **Amen.**

TENTH PRAYER

Our Father – Hail Mary.

O Jesus! Who art the beginning and end of all things,
life and virtue, remembers that for our sakes Thou was
plunged in an abyss of suffering from the soles of Thy
Feet to the crown of Thy Head.

In consideration of the enormity of Thy Wounds, teach me to keep, through pure love, Thy Commandments, whose way is wide and easy for those who love Thee. **Amen.**

ELEVENTH PRAYER

Our Father – Hail Mary.

O Jesus! Deep abyss of mercy, I beg of Thee, in memory of Thy Wounds which penetrated to the very marrow of Thy Bones and to the depth of Thy being, to draw me, a miserable sinner, overwhelmed by my offenses, away from sin and to hide me from Thy Face justly irritated against me, hide me in Thy wounds, until Thy anger and just indignation shall have passed away. **Amen.**

TWELFTH PRAYER

Our Father – Hail Mary.

O Jesus! Mirror of Truth, symbol of unity, bond of charity, remember the multitude of wounds with which Thou wast afflicted from head to foot, torn and reddened by the spilling of Thy adorable Blood. O great and universal pain, which Thou didst suffer in Thy virginal flesh for love of us! Sweetest Jesus! What is there that Thou couldst have done for us which Thou has not done!

May the fruit of Thy suffering be renewed in my soul by the faithful remembrance of Thy Passion, and may Thy love increase in my heart each day, until I see Thee in eternity: Thou Who art the treasure of every real good and every joy, which I beg Thee to grant me, O Sweetest Jesus, in heaven. **Amen.**

THIRTEENTH PRAYER
Our Father - Hail Mary.
O Jesus! Strong Lion, Immortal and Invincible King, remember the pain which Thou didst endure when all Thy strength, both moral and physical, was entirely exhausted, Thou didst bow Thy Head, saying: "It is consummated!"

Through this anguish and grief, I beg of Thee Lord

Jesus, to have mercy on me at the hour of my death when my mind will be greatly troubled and my soul will be in anguish. **Amen.**

FOURTEENTH PRAYER
Our Father – Hail Mary.
O Jesus! Only Son of the Father, Splendour and Figure of His Substance, remember the simple and humble recommendation.

Thou didst make of Thy Soul to Thy Eternal Father, saying: "Father, into Thy Hands I commend My Spirit!" And with Thy Body all torn, and Thy Heart Broken, and the bowels of Thy Mercy open to redeem us, Thou didst Expire.

By this Precious Death, I beg of Thee O King of Saints, comfort me and help me to resist the devil, the flesh and the world, so that being dead to the world I may live for Thee alone.

I beg of Thee at the hour of my death to receive me, a

pilgrim and an exile returning to Thee. **Amen.**

FIFTEENTH PRAYER

Our Father – Hail Mary.

O Jesus! True and fruitful Vine! Remember the abundant outpouring of Blood which Thou didst so generously shed from Thy Sacred Body as juice from grapes in a wine press.

From Thy Side, pierced with a lance by a soldier, blood and water issued forth until there was not left in Thy Body a single drop, and finally, like a bundle of myrrh lifted to the top of the Cross Thy delicate Flesh was destroyed, the very Substance of Thy Body withered, and the Marrow of Thy Bones dried up.

Through this bitter Passion and through the outpouring of Thy Precious Blood, I beg of Thee, O Sweet Jesus, to receive my soul when I am in my death agony. **Amen.**

CONCLUSION

O Sweet Jesus! Pierce my heart so that my tears of penitence and love will be my bread day and night; may I be converted entirely to Thee, may my heart be Thy perpetual habitation, may my conversation be pleasing to Thee, and may the end of my life be so praiseworthy that I may merit Heaven and there with Thy saints, praise Thee forever. **Amen.**